| DATE DUE | | | |
|----------|--|--|--|
| Mar18 '81 | | | |
| Oct 4 '81 | | | |
| Dec 11 '81 | | | |
| | | | |
| | | | |
| | | | |
| | | | |
| | | | |
| | | | |
| | | | |
| | | | |
| | | | |

# CHOOSING TOYS FOR CHILDREN

# CHOOSING TOYS FOR CHILDREN

## From Birth to Five

**Barbara Kaban**

**Illustrations by Diane Nicholls**

SCHOCKEN BOOKS • NEW YORK

First published by Schocken Books 1979

10 9 8 7 6 5 4 3 2 1     79 80 81 82

Copyright © 1979 by Schocken Books Inc.

**Library of Congress Cataloging in Publication Data**

Kaban, Barbara.
 Choosing toys for children.

 Bibliography: p.
 Includes index.
 1. Toys.    I. Title.
GV1218.5.K32     688.7′2     79–12628

Manufactured in the United States of America

to jody, jeff, and lenny

# CONTENTS

# Foreword

Anyone involved with young children—whether a professional worker in the child-care field or a new parent—is interested in the question of where toys and related materials fit into the child's developmental needs. Information about toys has traditionally been confusing and unreliable. In the last ten to fifteen years, however, our ability to select toys and to understand what makes one toy more appropriate than another, and which are the most fun, has grown substantially. Today we are in a much better position than ever before to deal with this subject.

We now know that when the infant's or young child's world meshes with his developing skills, not only does he move along a bit faster, but he seems to enjoy himself more and to develop a fuller taste for exploration, learning, and enjoyment. Therefore, good early child-rearing includes the provision of time and materials so the child is regularly involved in activities that interest him. We also know that 60 percent of the experience of babies appears to be nonsocial in orientation. While some of their waking time is spent eating, defending territory, or just idling, much of it—thousands of hours—is spent in interaction with objects large and small. As babies become toddlers and preschoolers, social skills develop. But they continue to be challenged by the physical content of their environment, and they spend long periods of time at play.

Looking at the larger process of the development of play during the early years of life, it seems to me that exploration or mastery tasks are examples of *learning how to learn*. Learning-to-learn activities are prerequisites or foundation skills. We can quite emphatically say that the play of young children constitutes a healthy percentage of the curriculum of early childhood. It has been my observation over the years that few commercially available toys have much of what we call "play value." Many of them are well constructed, but the bottom line (after safety issues) is whether or not the child will spend time with a toy beyond the initial novelty period. The information contained in this book will help toy buyers avoid wasting substantial amounts of time and money.

I am pleased to introduce this book by Barbara Kaban. She and I have worked together for thirteen years on the fascinating topic of how young children develop. As Assistant Director of the Harvard Preschool Project, she has an unusually long history of research experience with babies and young children. She has spent a huge amount of time in their homes, and has watched and tested what they actually can and cannot do, and what they enjoy doing. As a result, this book is an excellent source for well-founded information on the subject of choosing toys for children.

Burton L. White

# Preface

We have all experienced the shock and dismay of watching a child to whom we have just given a toy play happily with the box while ignoring the contents. This may be amusing at first, but soon we realize that we have wasted our money. Selecting a toy is not an easy task! We want to choose something that fulfills educational objectives, for psychologists and educators tell us that when children play they are learning basic concepts and developing problem-solving strategies. However, we also want something that is fun and will capture the child's interest.

Store shelves are stocked with a wide variety of toys for children from birth to age five. They all appear attractive, are labeled with suggested age ranges for their use, and may even claim to "teach" important skills. As toy buyers, what criteria should determine our selection? What is a good toy?

These are the questions I address in this book. It is written for any adult who wants to buy a toy for a child and who wants to spend his or her toy dollars wisely. Whether you are a parent, grandparent, aunt, uncle, baby-sitter, friend, or staff member of a nursery school or day-care center, you should be able to judge whether a toy is safe, interesting, and durable. Toy buyers should be able to assess the educational potential of a toy and be able to say with confidence, "This toy will be fun for a child to play with."

The chapters are organized to correspond to the growth and emerging toy needs of the child from birth to age five. Children progress rapidly in these early years, and the changes between twelve and twenty-four months are particularly dramatic. In addition, the emergence of negativism during the second year of life makes this period a trying one for many adults. A few well-chosen toys will not solve all the problems during these months but may make life somewhat easier for parent and child alike. Each chapter begins with a brief description of the skills and interests which emerge at that particular age to provide you with a framework for understanding my recommendations.

Which toys children play with and how frequently depends on the way in which adults display and store them. I have included a chapter on this important topic. Other topics that I cover are Books, Television, Alternative Toys, and Toys to Take When Traveling.

In each chapter I have alternated the use of the pronoun so that my reference to the child reads "she" in chapter 1, "he" in chapter 2, and so on. This does not mean that the toys in a specific chapter are appropriate only for a girl or only for a boy. It is simply my way of avoiding the use of "he or she" throughout the book. At no point are toys classified as "girl" toys or "boy" toys. This is a distinction which I have not found useful as a researcher or as a parent. Good toys match a child's interests and skills and may be enjoyed by either sex.

The recommendations in this book are based on knowledge I have acquired during thirteen years of research on the development of young children, as well as eight years of mothering experience. As Assistant Director of the Harvard Preschool Project, I visited hundreds of homes to observe the moment-to-moment activities of young children. I realized that, regardless of the financial circumstances of the home, parents placed a high priority on purchasing toys for their children. I saw some toys used in home after home while others were routinely ignored. Each year, during the holiday season, I watched children inundated with more toys, frequently receiving duplications of those they had previously ignored! This experience convinced me that too much money is spent on toys that do not match children's interests or skills. We need to learn to make more "informed" choices.

I cannot guarantee that every child will enjoy every toy described in this book, but I believe the book can increase the likelihood that your toy dollars will be spent wisely.

Barbara Kaban

# I
# Guidelines for Selecting Toys

Each year 5,000 new toys are introduced, and currently more than 150,000 are available to the American consumer. Only a small sample of the available toys are appropriate for children from birth to age five. I have chosen to review those toys which are readily available and meet the following criteria.

## Is the Toy Safe?

Although federal regulations exist to ensure minimum safety standards, it is impossible for government agencies to inspect every toy. Approximately 150,000 people were treated for injuries associated with toys in 1977, and during a three-month period in that year, 25 children under the age of three died from ingesting small parts of toys.

Before buying a toy, *inspect it*. The store should have a demonstration model available, so do not be put off by the fact that the toy is packaged. If you do not see an unwrapped model, ask for one.

Run your finger over the surface of the toy. Make sure there are no *sharp points* or *edges* that can cut or poke a child. Wooden toys should be expertly sanded to prevent painful splinters.

Children naturally inflict a fair amount of abuse on their toys, and good ones can take the punishment. See if the toy has squeakers, buttons, wheels, or other *small parts that may fall off if handled or manipulated frequently.* For children under the age of three, federal regulations define as hazardous any toy or piece of toy that is smaller than 1¼ inches in diameter and 2¼ inches in depth. Such small items may be swallowed or become lodged in a child's windpipe, ears, or nose.

Often a toy that is safe when intact becomes a serious hazard when cracked or missing a part. Broken toys expose dangerous points and sharp cutting edges. Animals and dolls are sometimes stuffed with small pellets. If a seam opens, the pellets can be swallowed or inhaled. The same hazard can occur with a broken rattle or musical toy. Inspect toys regularly and remove damaged items.

Children under the age of five put most things in their mouth. The paints and dyes used to decorate toys should be *nontoxic.* This is particularly important when considering the purchase of antique toys or those made outside the United States.

## Is the Toy Washable?

Toys that are loved are handled a great deal and get dirty. A toy that is not easily cleaned can become a health hazard long before its usefulness has diminished.

## Will the Toy Last?

A good toy should be able to withstand fingering, mouthing, banging, hammering, and occasionally being stepped on without falling apart. These behaviors all fall within the range of normal abuse that children inflict on toys. Manufacturers know this, and good toys are designed to withstand innovative methods of play. Buttons, levers, switches and pull strings should be designed so that they cannot be dislodged or broken easily.

Cost does not necessarily reflect quality in design or

construction, but there are times when a costlier version is the more economical choice in the long run. After buying a third set of plastic dishes in five years, I realized I had spent more than if I had bought the costlier but sturdier aluminum version in the first place. Toys made out of heavy-duty plastic, wood, or metal last longer. Good toys are designed to span several years in the life of a child and should be available to be passed down to a younger sibling.

## Is the Toy Interesting?

All toys have initial novelty value. Good toys are ones that children come back to over and over again. Children are interested in toys that they can do something to or with. Toys that "perform" and leave the child to be the audience are not good choices for children beyond infancy. Children prefer toys that they can manipulate and that allow them to practice new skills. Toys that encourage children to discover how things work or what they themselves are capable of doing are good choices.

## Is the Toy Aesthetically Pleasing to Children?

What appeals to adults does not necessarily appeal to children, and most toys in the birth to five-year age range are designed to appeal to the adult toy buyer. I learned this lesson most emphatically from my son. I had purchased a beautiful set of natural wood cars. One day I found him industriously painting them. When asked what he was doing, he replied, "I'm finishing them. No one ever finished them." Generally, children like brightly colored, uncluttered toys.

## Will the Toy Cause Frustration or Boredom?

Toys that are too easy or too difficult are inappropriate selections. Children enjoy a sense of mastery over their environment but are not fooled by tasks which offer no challenge. Unfortunately, manufacturers frequently label toys "up," and unsuspecting adults purchase toys that may bore the older child. (An example of this is the Surprise Box, an excellent mastery toy for the ten- to eighteen-month-old. The manufacturer, however, recommends it for the two- to four-year-old.) Toys that demand skills your child does not yet have or that contain buttons or levers that are too difficult for a child to operate independently will result in frustration (and often the destruction of the toy). Understanding which skills your child has already mastered and which are emerging is essential for successfully selecting toys.

## Can the Child Use the Toy Alone?

If a toy requires adult participation, make sure this is an activity you enjoy doing with the child or else she will not get to play with the toy. Many toys will require a brief demonstration, but they should not require continuous adult participation. If this is the case with most of the toys you buy, you are not making good choices.

## Of What Educational Value Is the Toy?

In recent years, newspaper and magazine articles, books, and television have sensitized us to the educational importance of the years before a child enters elementary school. Previously, the popular sentiment was that children began their education when they entered first grade. Now it is generally recognized that learning begins at birth and that the successful completion of the "curriculum" of the first five years is essential for continued achievement. Parents, then, are the children's earliest educators, and the materials they provide become the learning tools for the young child.

Most toys for children from birth to age five are

designed to encourage eye-hand coordination, large-muscle coordination, concept development, or imagination and pretending. These categories represent the emerging motor and intellectual skills which shape young children's interests and abilities and provide a useful classification system for understanding the different purposes toys may serve.

The first category of toys includes things such as baby's first mobile (although she only looks at it) and moves up through the age range to include stacking rings, beads for stringing, and sewing cards. These toys encourage the development of eye-hand coordination, which begins with looking and reaching and leads to mastery tasks requiring skillful fine motor coordination. They are tasks the child uses to practice her skills, and at this time she is more concerned with the process than the product.

The second category includes those activities which encourage the child to master the use of her body. Children enjoy the challenge of mastering emerging skills and will practice them over and over again. A baby who has learned to pull herself to a standing position will drop down and repeat the procedure over and over. This same dedication, tenacity, and pride will be observed in a child learning to ride a tricycle, throw a ball, or climb a jungle gym.

The third category consists of toys that teach basic concepts such as size, shape, or color, or require problem-solving strategies for their completion. These toys encourage children to plan and carry out multistepped sequences, to note similarities and differences, and to anticipate consequences. Shape sorters, puzzles, and blocks are a few examples of toys in this category.

The fourth category consists of toys designed to encourage imagination and pretending. Imitation of adult actions or statements are usually the first forms of "pretend" behavior we observe in young children. Pretending blossoms more fully at about two years of age and continues throughout childhood. Probably no other category of play makes adults more uncomfortable. I have been asked by parents, "Should I discourage pretending? Will my child be able to differentiate reality from fantasy if she pretends too much?" Our research showed that children who were developing well spent more time in pretend activities than children who were developing poorly. They used pretending as a way of "trying on" adult behaviors. Pretending can also provide a socially acceptable avenue for the expression of negative feelings, as well as an opportunity to work through feelings about traumatic events. Adults can use pretend activities to familiarize children with an unfamiliar event, such as going to the doctor's office. Pretending does not require expensive costumes or equipment. A child's imagination can turn one feather into a full Indian costume. However, several items seem to appeal to most children, starting with a toy telephone, and appropriate recommendations will be made throughout the age range.

Another category that overlaps all of the above is arts and crafts. This category refers to activities which encourage the exploration of different media. Children can be introduced to these creative processes long before many adults anticipate. An eighteen-month-old will delight in modeling dough, and experimentation with crayons, markers, and paint can begin as early as two. Beginning at eighteen months I recommend a series of materials and toys which make arts and crafts activities easy and fun.

All of these categories are useful to have in mind when selecting toys for young children, but it is important to remember that most toys encompass more than one skill or ability. For example, stacking rings encourages eye-hand coordination in the twelve-month-old but may be used as a vehicle for learning about size gradations for the eighteen-month-old. By age four, these labels become increasingly difficult to apply since the integration of these discrete abilities now allows the child to function at a more complex level.

## Is the Toy Fun?

Sometimes in our enthusiasm to provide the best environment for a child we forget the most basic fact. No toy, no matter how durable, safe, or educational will be used unless it is *fun*. Adult attitudes toward toys often affect their play value for children. If a toy is so costly or so fragile that adults become anxious when a child manipulates it, the toy is no longer "fun." If adults insist there is only one correct way to use a toy, it is no longer "fun." Children delight in the unexpected, the unusual, and the absurd when they play. A child left to her own devices will enjoy toys in ways adults never anticipate. A good toy stimulates the child's curiosity and creativity and should also be fun for the adult care giver because children enjoy sharing their toys with those they love.

Each child develops skills at her own pace. Some two-year-olds are particularly adept at tasks that require fine motor coordination. Other well-developing two-year-olds may not be able to master a "fine motor" toy that I have recommended for an eighteen-month-old. My recommendations are approximations of when most children will enjoy a particular toy. Observe the child carefully to determine her interests and capabilities. In some instances you may want to put a toy away for three to six months; in other instances you may have to look ahead to the next chapter to find a toy which will excite and challenge the child.

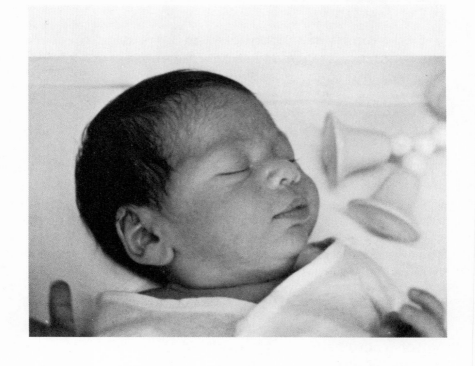

## II

# Birth to Crawling

There is no greater stimulus to buy toys than the presence of a newborn. Miniature footballs, dolls, stuffed animals, extravagant mobiles, crib gyms, and colorful infant paraphernalia are all hard to resist. But what is the newborn likely to use?

Infants differ in temperament; some of them seem to sleep all the time, while others are awake more than their parents thought possible. Regardless of individual behavior, the newborn is not interested in toys. All his energy is devoted to eating, sleeping, and soliciting comfort from those who care for him. By four weeks of age, the baby has brief periods when he is content and alert. During these periods he begins to enjoy the movement and music provided by a colorful mobile.

By three months of age, the baby's delight in his mobile will be evident. His coos and laughter frequently can be heard in the next room. But now he is ready to do more than just look at an interesting mobile. When objects are placed close enough, he will reach out for them. Now is the time for a good crib gym, which will reward the baby with a sound or the movement of an interesting object. Does the baby "know" he is making things happen? Not really. He is still too young to think: "If I do this, then that will happen"; but he is learning.

A baby learns about the world through his senses. He touches, tastes and smells the objects he comes in contact with and is most content when he is gumming something. A good teething ring that is easy to grasp and interesting to look at will quickly become a favorite toy. However, should the teether fall, the baby will make no attempt to find it or express displeasure at its loss. At this age, out of sight means out of mind.

Every newborn receives at least one rattle. Unfortunately, this traditional gift is rarely appealing to or appropriate for the infant. During the first three months of life, the baby will keep his hands closed tightly in a fist. If you pry his fingers open and place the rattle in his hand, he shows little interest in its presence. Some rattles are meant to be teethers also (and some even contain mirrors), but they are too bulky to be gummed comfortably by the older baby. Rattles rarely hold a baby's interest, even for a brief period.

When the baby can sit up, he is ready for a new group of toys. Cloth blocks and a clutch ball are good choices. They are easy to grasp, light enough to be thrown or pushed with little effort, and soft enough for the baby to topple on safely. "Activity centers" and pull-string toys that attach to the sides of a crib or playpen are frequently purchased for babies in this age range. These toys offer a simple response for the baby's actions (e.g., a bell rings when he pushes a button or music plays when he pulls a string), but they do not hold the infant's interest beyond the initial novelty. The responses these toys offer quickly become boring to the baby, especially when compared with the discoveries he makes moving about the house.

When the baby begins to crawl, both his life and yours change dramatically. He can now touch all the things he has been looking at for the past nine months. Suddenly parents find that neither baby nor household items stay where they are put anymore. His curiosity is insatiable. Everything exists to be touched, tasted, banged, and thrown whether it is a soft cloth block or a fragile family heirloom. Electric outlets, extension cords, plants, detergents, and cleansers are just a partial list of common and potentially lethal household objects that occupy the same space the baby is busily exploring.* Parents must examine their home through the eyes of this inexperienced explorer and remove hazardous objects. Remember, to a baby, all objects are new, exciting, and safe.

Once a baby masters crawling, he has achieved one of the dramatic milestones in his young life. His interests and toy needs are now similar to those of the one-year-old rather than the infant. Before making that transition, let's take a closer look at the recommended toys for infants. The list, however, is brief. The period from birth to crawling is not the time to invest heavily in toys.

## Mobiles: Airplane Musical Mobile by Eden

A mobile provides visual stimulation for the infant. Unfortunately, most mobiles are designed to appeal to the adults who buy them rather than the infants who use them. Try this experiment. Look up at a mobile as if you were an infant. If all you can see is the bottom edge of the

---

*A discussion of practices and strategies for childproofing a home can be found in chapter 10, Display and Storage of Toys.

attractive figures, the mobile was not designed with the infant's needs in mind.

Mobiles vary in cost and complexity. Some move only when a gentle breeze blows, and others have mechanisms that allow them to rotate while playing a lullaby. The newborn is attracted by movement, is soothed by music, and prefers brightly colored objects. The Airplane Musical Mobile by Eden is one of the few available mobiles that incorporates all of these features.

In order for a mobile to be effective, it must be positioned correctly. Between the ages of four weeks and fourteen weeks, an infant looks to his right 80 percent of the time. The mobile should hang over the right side of the crib and the figures should be approximately fourteen inches above the surface of the mattress.

Warning: Mobiles should be removed from the crib when the baby begins to sit up. Mobiles are not constructed to withstand tugs or support the weight of a baby who is pulling himself up. Serious injuries could occur.

## Crib Gyms: Play Gym by Fisher-Price

Crib gyms are toys attached to a bar that spans the width of the crib or playpen. Crib gyms are also called "activators" or "entertainers." Regardless of their name, the purpose of a crib gym is to encourage hand-eye coordination in the infant. Crib gyms differ in complexity. Some will provide an interesting sound or movement with the slightest contact. Others require fairly sophisticated action from the infant in order to make something happen.

Most manufacturers recommend crib gyms for children from three months to eighteen months of age. In my experience, their usefulness diminishes dramatically once the baby can sit up. Crib gyms are designed for use by an infant who is lying on his back. A child who can sit up will not be content in the supine position for any length of time. For this reason you should purchase a crib gym that is geared to the abilities of the three- to seven-month-old. The most effective crib gym for a child in this age range is one that offers a response to the slightest touch.

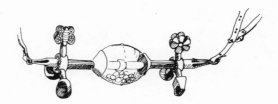

The Fisher-Price Play Gym is an excellent version of this toy. The objects hanging down from the bar are attached to rigid support arms. (If objects are attached to the bar by a string, the baby's clumsy motions tend to push the objects out of his reach. It is similar to an adult's trying to grasp a light string in a dark closet.) The large transparent ball filled with brightly colored beads twirls easily, producing interesting sounds and movement. The crib gym is sturdy and will easily withstand all the grasping and batting activity a baby directs at it. Priced competitively with other name-brand "gyms," the Fisher-Price model is better suited to the abilities of the three- to seven-month-old baby.

## Mirrors: Baby Mirror by Childcraft

We all find it hard to ignore our own reflection in a mirror. Even though a baby will not recognize himself, he, too, will be intrigued by what he sees. Each time he looks, he sees a face that changes its expression and moves.

A baby mirror should not be made of glass. A high-quality stainless steel mirror provides an image that is not distorted and will not break when dropped. The Childcraft Baby Mirror is a two-sided, moderately priced mirror. Its plastic frame has six "finger" holes, which make it easy to hang on the side of a crib and easy for a baby to grasp and carry when he is older.

## Teethers: Space Ring Teether and Three Teethers by Creative Playthings

Any time a baby is cranky, someone will offer the explanation "He must be teething." Whether his gums are bothering him or not, a baby will enjoy playing with teething rings. Teethers come in a wide assortment of colors, shapes, and prices. They are made out of wood, plastic, or rubber and are designed to be gummed. A good teether should be easy to grasp and interesting to look at.

The Space Ring Teether consists of three brightly colored concentric circles. It is made out of hard molded plastic and is easy for a baby to grasp with one or both hands. Three Teethers is a set of three soft plastic teethers. Each brightly colored teether is 3⅓ inches in diameter and has a slight variation in texture and shape.

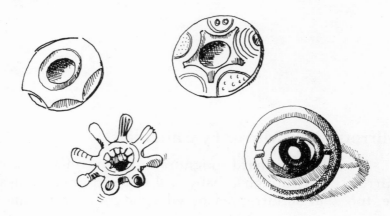

All four are constructed to withstand extensive handling and dropping. They are easy to wash and do not contain little parts that can break off and become a hazard. Rather than trying to incorporate every feature that is supposed to appeal to babies (e.g., rattles and mirrors), the Creative Playthings teethers are simple, efficient toys that will please a baby.

## Cloth Blocks by Childcraft

Once your baby can sit up unaided, cloth blocks are a good toy. They are easy to grasp, interesting to look at, and easy to stack. Although the novice builder will rarely stack more than two blocks, should he succeed in building a tower, he will not get hurt when it topples. In fact, the more enjoyable aspect of building for the young child is to knock over the tower he has (or you have) created.

The Cloth Blocks by Childcraft are soft, washable foam cubes, each 3¾ inches. Other versions of cloth blocks are made by Creative Playthings, Knickerbocker, and Child Guidance Toys. A vinyl version is made by Dolly Toys. The sets vary in the number of blocks each contains. For example, Creative Playthings offers nine blocks and consequently costs more than the Childcraft set of six blocks. This is one instance where less is sufficient. Six blocks will adequately serve the needs of the young builder. The quantity, quality, and price of the Childcraft product makes it the best choice.

## Stuffed Animals

We all remember a favorite stuffed animal that we slept with each night when we were young. Although this special relationship usually does not emerge until sometime around the second birthday, the stuffed animal

that becomes the focus for this attention is usually purchased during a baby's early months.

A good stuffed animal is sturdy enough to withstand tight squeezes, rough handling, and lots of loving. The materials used in its construction should be flame-resistant and washable. The dyes used must be nontoxic. The eyes and ears should be firmly anchored and contain no metal connecting wires. The fur should not shed. Stuffed animals can be too small or too large for carrying and cuddling. The best size is between eight and twelve inches in height.

Again, trying to incorporate every feature that might appeal to a child (or, more likely, the adult who is making the purchase), many manufacturers offer musical stuffed animals. The music box will not be an asset from the child's point of view. The mechanism makes the animal less flexible and not as suitable for cuddling.

I recommend the stuffed animals made by Steiff. Although more expensive, the Steiff animals are sturdy, made of high-quality materials, and appealing; they have been known to be passed down from one generation to the next. Bears, dogs, monkeys, elephants, cats, and rabbits are just a small sample of the wide variety of animals Steiff offers.

## Baby Clutch Ball by Creative Playthings

Balls are consistently one of the most popular toys throughout childhood. When your baby learns to sit up and begins to move around, a ball is an exciting toy to push and chase.

The Creative Playthings Clutch Ball is well designed for the six- to twelve-month-old child. It is 5½ inches in diameter and made of soft, flexible rubber. Rather than being perfectly round, its surface has been cut out to form "handles" that make the ball easier for a baby to grasp and to carry. Although the ball rolls when pushed gently, it comes to a stop quickly and is more likely to stay still as inexperienced hands try to grasp it. The Clutch Ball is light enough to be lifted and thrown and soft enough to act as a gentle cushion should the baby fall over on it.

# III

# One Year to Eighteen Months Old

The one-year-old child is a charmer. She smiles at anyone who glances her way but withdraws shyly when a stranger approaches too closely. She knows when she is the center of attention and delights in the admiration that is justifiably hers. The "ohs" and "ahs" of grandparents, aunts, uncles, and cousins prompt her to perform, sometimes resulting in clownish behavior. She will clap and laugh enthusiastically with her audience just to be one of the group, although it is clear she has little understanding of what is really happening.

The one-year-old child's foremost interest is mastering the ability to walk. Her first steps are hesitant but increase rapidly in frequency, number, and skill. With each step, her pride in her accomplishment can be seen in her smile and the way she glances for approval from attending adults. When taking those first steps, she must work hard to maintain her balance and uses the trick of all good ballet dancers: holding her hands out away from her body. The transition from crawling to walking is gradual and takes several months to be complete. In the interim, when in a hurry, she will revert to the ease and speed of being on all fours.

Like a mountain climber whose reason for climbing is that "the mountain is there," the one-year-old cannot resist a staircase. The opportunity to practice going up and down (and frequently switching directions halfway) never seems to bore or tire her. Although most one-year-olds have mastered the art of going up, descending must still be practiced. Even if a child appears proficient, she should not be allowed on steps without supervision.

Mastering other large motor skills such as riding four-wheeled vehicles and throwing balls also intrigues the one-year-old child. In fact, throwing balls, blocks, bottles, and food are all challenging and pleasurable to the child. Throwing toys and expecting others to retrieve them quickly evolves into a favorite pastime.

Another critical developmental area that blossoms around the child's first birthday is the ability to understand words. Although the child does not use language to express her feelings and needs, she is beginning to associate labels with objects and names with people. The first words she learns are those the people around her use every day: Mommy, Daddy, spoon, cup, bottle, bye-bye. She also is beginning to understand simple directions such as "Get your bottle" or "Wave bye-bye." By the time she is three, the child will understand most of the words used in everyday adult conversation.

To a child in this age range, books are just one of many new objects to explore. She is too young to listen to a story, but she enjoys flipping the pages of the book. At times she will be patient enough to allow you to supply the names for the familiar objects and animals depicted, but on other occasions she will breeze through the book so quickly that you will barely catch a glimpse of the pictures.

Children in this age range love hinged objects. Opening and closing a door and manipulating the Gabriel Surprise Box appeal to this budding mechanic. In addition, emptying containers, boxes, and drawers is frequently more interesting than playing with the contents.

The one-year-old child is still highly distractible and will gladly accept one toy in place of another should the need arise. Her cooperative disposition will not last long, so take advantage of its presence and distract her away from unacceptable pursuits by offering an appropriate toy. It is also a good time to teach older siblings to employ this strategy. Once a baby can move around by herself, nothing is safe from her scrutiny. An older sibling may find this intrusion particularly painful. Teaching an older child how to remove a treasured object from the hands of a one-year-old child is more effective than trying to explain that the one-year-old meant no harm. One wise four-year-old was heard counseling a friend, "You can take *anything* from her as long as you give her something else first."

Everything is new, exciting, and interesting to the one-year-old. Most toys will have initial novelty value, but only a few will hold the child's interest for more than a brief period of time.

## Riding Horse by Fisher-Price

A riding toy for a one-year-old child must be a well-balanced, easy-to-mount vehicle. In addition, the toy must be correctly proportioned for the child or it becomes a safety hazard. If the vehicle is too tall or too wide, it will topple as the child tries to get on and off. If her feet do not rest flat on the floor when she is seated, she will be unable to make it move.

The Fisher-Price Riding Horse has several attractive features that make it preferable over other four-wheeled riding toys. It is sturdily constructed of heavy-duty molded plastic and has wide track wheels that keep it steady. It is attractively painted in red, white, and blue and makes an appealing "clippity clop" sound as the wheels turn. In addition, a tug on the reins produces a definite "whinny" response from the horse. The back of the seat has a handle that is useful for grasping and serves as a backstop to prevent the enthusiastic equestrian from sliding off her horse. And finally, there is a handy storage tray that enables the child to take her favorite toys along for a ride. The Riding Horse, priced competitively with other four-wheeled vehicles, is an interesting toy for the one-year-old child to explore as well as to use for practicing her newly acquired gross motor skills.

## Surprise Box by Gabriel

The Surprise Box is recommended by the manufacturer for children between two and four years of age but has the greatest play appeal between ten and eighteen months. This toy combines several mechanical operations that intrigue the young child. It consists of five switches, which the child pushes, turns, or pulls to make a door open and a figure pop up. The little doors snap closed easily and, unlike a Jack-in-the-box, can be manipulated by a child without the aid of an adult. Most Jack-in-the-box toys require that the child hold down the clown with one hand, close the lid with the other hand, and pull out the hand holding the clown at the strategic moment so that the lid snaps shut without catching her fingers. This complex sequence is beyond most one-year-old children.

Children vary in their ability to operate the different switches on the Surprise Box, but most find the light switch the easiest to master. By eighteen months of age, a child's fine motor skills will be more fully developed and she will be able to activate all of the switches. This toy is sturdy and will withstand being dropped or stepped on more than once. The intrinsic appeal of the Surprise Box makes it an excellent toy to offer to a child when you need a few uninterrupted moments to complete a task or have a cup of coffee.

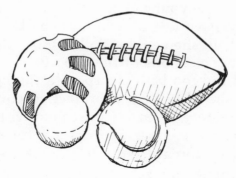

## Balls

Movement attracts and intrigues the one-year-old child, and nothing moves more easily than a lightweight ball. Balls roll, bounce, and sail through the air and come in a wide variety of colors, sizes, shapes, and textures. All of these characteristics make the ball one of the most popular toys throughout childhood.

There are many inexpensive, brightly colored balls available in toy stores, supermarkets, and drugstores. For the one-year-old child, a ball should not be too large (more than nine inches in diameter) or too small (able to fit in her mouth). Beach balls, tennis balls, and rubber balls appeal to children. However, the one-year-old is more likely to use a ball indoors and has little concept of the damage or harm that can result when a ball collides with an object or a person. Consequently, the best ball for a child in this age range is the Wiffle Ball. These lightweight, hollow plastic balls are easy to throw, roll, and grasp and are too light to harm whatever they hit. Wiffle Balls come in two sizes: regulation baseball size and the larger, regulation softball size. Each can be purchased for less than one dollar and are well worth the investment.

Parker Brothers makes a series of soft foam balls called Nerf Balls. They come in a variety of sizes and shapes. Two popular versions for children of this age are the seven-inch Super Nerf Ball and the smaller Junior Nerf Ball. These round, soft balls are perfect for indoor use and easy for the young child to grasp and manipulate. However, they have one serious drawback: Should the child bite the ball, she could dislodge small pieces of the soft foam. Other versions of the Nerf Balls, such as the basketball and the football, incorporate the lightweight, soft qualities and also have a protective covering that eliminates the safety hazard. Consequently, the basketball and football are more appropriate for the young child who still explores most objects with her mouth.

Another intriguing set of balls for a child is the Protour practice golf balls. Although not originally designed for children, these small, hollow balls are fun to roll and retrieve and make a delightful sound when they are bounced on a hard wood floor. They come six to a package and cost less than one dollar.

## Letter Wooden Blocks by Playskool

Small wooden blocks are easy for the one-year-old child to grasp and stack. The Playskool sets come in

sturdy storage containers that enable a child to partake in her favorite activity: dumping the contents out of the can.

Playskool offers a wide assortment of small wooden blocks to choose from: letter blocks, number blocks, blocks with Disney characters, and blocks with Sesame Street characters. The sets range in contents from sixteen to fifty natural wood finish blocks, each $1\frac{5}{16}$ inches. Each block has a picture embossed on two sides and printed on four sides, but children in this age range rarely attend to the decorative characters. The smaller letter and number sets are sufficient to satisfy the building needs of a one-year-old. She will not make elaborate structures. In fact, stacking three blocks is an achievement, but she will delight in knocking over the tall towers you construct for her.

## Rock-a-Stack by Fisher-Price

Toys frequently appeal to children for different reasons than they appeal to adults. The Rock-a-Stack is such a toy. It consists of six brightly colored plastic rings, graduated in size, which fit over a tapered cone. Adults buy this toy because it appears to teach color and size concepts. The one-year-old child likes it because the rings are delightful to chew, easy to grasp, and light enough to carry as she moves around the house. She is attracted to

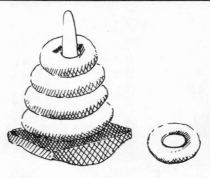

the bright colors and enjoys removing the rings from the cone but rarely restacks them correctly. In fact, the sophisticated size and color gradations are wasted on the one-year-old child. (By the time the child is two, she will easily master the size sequencing but will not find this toy as appealing as she did when younger.) Other versions of this toy are made out of wood or offer a larger cone with more rings. However, more rings are not necessary, and wooden rings are not as pleasant to chew. The Fisher-Price Rock-a-Stack is a moderately priced toy that a child will enjoy.

## Bath Toys: Milk Carrier and Floating Family by Fisher-Price

Most one-year-old children love bathtime. Pouring water, fishing for the soap, and experimenting with splashing, sliding, and "swimming" are just a few of the activities they find amusing. Manufacturers have provided a broad array of toys to augment a child's bathtime activities. They range from simple rubber animals to elaborate mechanisms that hook over the side of the tub and spout water in addition to doing other tricks.

I prefer simple toys that allow children to follow their own inclinations and naturally discover the vast play potential of water. Two such toys are the Milk Carrier and the Floating Family by Fisher-Price.

The Milk Carrier, shown here, is one of the less expensive and more versatile toys on the market. A long-time favorite, it consists of six plastic containers shaped like old-fashioned milk bottles. Each bottle is 5¼ inches high and has a flip-top lid. Four of the bottles are white, one is orange, and one is brown (chocolate milk, anyone?). These bottles are perfect for water and sand play and become delightful props in dramatic play episodes as the child gets older.

The Floating Family is a six-piece set consisting of three large figures (each $3^7/_{16}$ inches high), a turtle, a boat, and a pitcher. All are made of durable plastic and float easily. The figures and pitcher are weighted so that they bob and upright themselves in water. The figures are designed to sit in the boat and the turtle and fit easily into the pitcher, too. The six pieces are easy to grasp and incorporate in one set the best features of pouring and floating toys.

## First Books

At first, books are just one more interesting toy to explore rather than a source of pictures and words.

Consequently, they must be sturdy enough to withstand being mouthed, dropped, and carried around unceremoniously by the tip of one page. The best type of book for a child of this age is one with thick cardboard pages. The child will enjoy flipping the pages back and forth and will gradually begin to attend to the pictures. The illustrations should be bright and bold and should depict familiar objects and animals. "Reading" to the child will consist of supplying the correct label for the picture. It will be awhile before she will have the interest, understanding, and patience required to listen to a real story.

There are many cardboard-paged books available in toy and book stores. One of my favorites is Richard Scarry's *Early Words*. Many other appropriate "first" books are available, and most can be purchased for less than three dollars. Two or three cardboard-paged books will be a satisfactory beginning for your child's personal library.

# IV

# Eighteen Months to Two Years Old

Now that the child has mastered the basic physical skills of walking, running, and climbing (although he will continue to refine and expand these abilities throughout childhood), he turns his attention to one of the most important areas of his life: his relationship with his parents. Somewhere between sixteen and twenty-four months, the child begins to realize that he is a separate individual with his own likes and dislikes. He expresses this growing awareness by adamantly asserting his will and testing previously accepted limits. If he does not get his way, he cries, screams, kicks, and thrashes about. This type of behavior is commonly referred to as the "terrible twos."

Fortunately, this is only a phase from which most children emerge sometime after their second birthday. However, a child in the midst of this difficult developmental period will say no to most offers and suggestions even when he really means yes. The child's newly acquired sense of autonomy prompts him to test the limits of that autonomy. Although this is frequently a stressful and irritating time for parents, it is important to remember that this behavior is a normal and important part of growing up.

The most effective strategy is to set clear, firm limits and enforce them consistently. It also helps to let the child win some of the less important struggles once in a while. Although toys cannot solve any of the problems you may be experiencing during this period, a selection of appropriate toys may provide an acceptable outlet for the child's energy and interests.

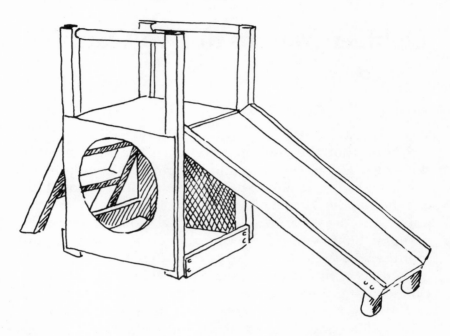

## Indoor Gym House by Creative Playthings

Mastering gross motor skills builds a sense of confidence and pride in one's accomplishments. The Creative Playthings Indoor Gym House challenges the toddler to attempt new feats in addition to practicing previously acquired skills. This well-designed, carefully constructed toy is appropriately scaled in size for use by the young child.

The Indoor Gym consists of a three-step ladder that is easy to climb and a short (36 inches), wide slide that is ideal for the eighteen-month-old child. Before long he will be sliding down headfirst and climbing up the slide instead of the ladder. This unique toy also has a crawl space under the platform, a perfect "private corner" for thinking, hiding, or storing special toys. This Indoor Gym will be used for many years by the child and his friends.

## Hammering Toys: Cobbler's Bench by Playskool

Hammering is one of the exploratory strategies to which children subject all toys. This classic wooden pounding bench, built to withstand the roughest hammering, encourages hand-eye coordination while offering a constructive outlet for this behavior. The Playskool Cobbler's Bench comes with a mallet and six brightly colored pegs. The child can pound as hard as he likes, enjoying the force of his strikes, the loud noise which results, and the obvious movement of the pegs. When the pegs are nearly through, he just flips the bench over and starts pounding again.

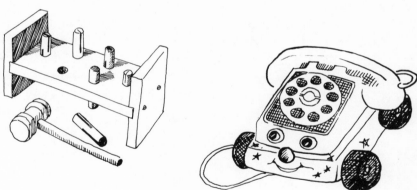

## Chatter Telephone by Fisher-Price

Telephones intrigue the young child. The sense of wonder invoked by hearing a familiar voice without seeing the person is greater than any trick performed by a magician. Some of the earliest role-playing episodes I have observed were of toddlers imitating adult mannerisms and inflections when talking on the telephone. The "pretend" possibilities of talking to Daddy when he is at work or a grandma who lives in a distant city delight the young child.

The Fisher-Price Chatter Telephone is designed to stand up to the use and abuse of a toddler. The wide plastic wheels protect the telephone as the eighteen-month-old unceremoniously transports it from one location to another.

## Puzzles by Playskool and Fisher-Price

Solving puzzles requires hand-eye coordination, perceptual discrimination, and information about size and color relationships. The eighteen-month-old child is ready for his first puzzle, but it must be carefully selected so that he may master it successfully. Playskool offers an excellent selection of beginner puzzles. These four- and five-piece wooden inlay puzzles depict subjects familiar to young children. Each piece is a complete picture of an object, painted in bright, nontoxic colors, and is large enough to be easily manipulated by small hands.

Fisher-Price offers a slightly more advanced assortment of wooden puzzles. These puzzles, consisting of six to thirteen pieces, have two unique features: an easy-lift

knob located in the center of each piece and a surprise picture under each puzzle piece.

Being able to complete a puzzle successfully is a rewarding experience for the young child, and he enjoys doing the same puzzle over and over again. Soon, however, he will be ready to move on to more complex puzzles, which require putting pieces together to form a complete picture.

## Pull Toys: Rattle Ball by Fisher-Price

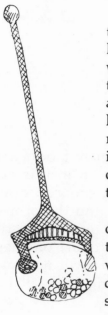

A toddler loves to carry and pull large toys as he moves around the house. Recognizing this, manufacturers offer a wide variety of "pull toys" to accompany the child in his travels. Many consist of appealing animals attached to a string. I prefer pull toys consisting of a wooden rod attached to a base that makes noise as it moves. The wooden rod will not break, catch on furniture, or get wrapped around the toddler's leg.

The Fisher-Price Rattle Ball consists of wooden balls that "rattle" as they tumble inside the plastic globe. Other versions have figures that pop up and down or chime units that produce musical sounds. The Fisher-Price pull toys vary considerably in price. Basically, they all serve the same purpose: to provide a safe toy for a child to pull or push as he walks. Consequently, this is one instance where the least expensive model is certainly adequate.

## Shape Sorting Box by Creative Playthings

The Shape Sorting Box is a three-dimensional puzzle. It is a durable plastic box whose hinged top has five openings of different shapes; ten colorful wooden blocks (two of each shape) fit into the openings. First the child must differentiate one shape from another. Then he must match the block to the appropriate opening. Finally, he must position the block correctly if it is to slide into the box. If introduced correctly, the Shape Sorting Box is a challenging learning experience rather than an over-whelming task.

At first, it is best to limit the number of blocks and shapes the child is working with. Children in this age range are most familiar with circles and squares. Start with one of each and allow the child to find the proper opening through trial and error. He will quickly master this preliminary stage. Then you may introduce one new shape at a time. This phasing-in process will not take long, and soon the child will be working with all ten pieces.

## Play Family by Fisher-Price

The Fisher-Price Play Family consists of men, women, children, workers, pets and animals. These delightful wooden and plastic figures inhabit the attractive and cleverly designed house, village, school, farm, hospital, garage, airport, and castle offered by the manufacturer. Each environment comes with the appropriate furniture, cars, trucks, and equipment, and the little people are designed to sit comfortably in their vehicles or chairs. No child needs all of these toys, and most would be satisfied with the little people and accessories offered in one of the following utility sets.

## Play Family House Bath Utility Set

This set consists of four people and eight pieces of furniture: washer, dryer, sewing machine, chair, bathroom scale, bathtub, vanity, and toilet with a lid that opens and closes. Children enjoy playing with the miniature appliances and furniture they see every day in their own homes. A child in the midst of toilet training will be particularly fascinated by the Bath Utility Set and will act out many of his own experiences.

## Play Family Nursery Set

This set consists of four people and six pieces of furniture: playpen, high chair, cradle, stroller, rocking horse, and dressing table. Each figure fits into the pieces of furniture and both the rocking horse and the stroller have rotating wheels.

## Play Family Little Riders

This seven-piece set consists of two people and five vehicles: airplane, truck, train engine, tricycle, and riding horse. The figures fit in the vehicles, and each vehicle has rotating wheels and other movable parts.

## Pail and Shovel

Once the warm weather has arrived, a toddler enjoys digging in his own backyard, in a sandbox, or at the beach. Filling a pail with sand, dumping the contents, and starting over again is a simple, redundant task that delights the eighteen-month-old child. Manufacturers

offer a wide variety of pails, shovels, rakes, sand molds, and sand wheels, but all the eighteen-month-old child needs is a simple pail and shovel. In this case, purchasing the least expensive model you can find makes the most sense. Children in this age range misplace or bury their tools, and you will find yourself buying replacements.

## Play Doh by Kenner

Touching, poking, pounding, and pulling are natural exploratory behaviors for the eighteen-month-old child and nowhere are they more appropriately applied than when using Play Doh by Kenner. This soft, pliable dough comes in four bright, nontoxic colors. It can be rolled, pounded, cut, and shaped again and again. Although an eighteen-month-old child may not be interested in cutting out shapes or making objects, he will enjoy manipulating this dough, which feels and smells so good.

Play Doh comes in a variety of sizes: a one-ounce can, which makes an excellent party favor; a set of four six-ounce cans; and a large three-pound can. The best size for home use is the set of four cans. For a modest cost, Play Doh is a delightful and creative medium.*

*Modeling dough can also be made at home. See chapter 8, Alternative Toys.

# V

# Two to Three Years Old

As the contentiousness of the "terrible twos" subsides, a more cooperative child emerges. However, she has her own distinct style and preferences. Some two-year-old children are more physical than others and are "on the go" every minute of the day. For this child, engaging in large-muscle activities—such as running, climbing, sliding, riding a four-wheeled toy, or spinning on a Sit and Spin—dominates her waking hours. Other two-year-olds are able to sit still long enough to string beads, fill a board with pegs, build with blocks, or "write" with crayons. Regardless of the child's style, she is more interested in *mastering the process* than in the product that results from her actions. Although she engages in each activity for a relatively brief period of time, she enjoys practicing the required skills and comes back to each activity again and again.

Another activity that blossoms during the third year of life is dramatic play. The child acts out the adult roles she is most familiar with, such as parent, bus driver, or construction worker. Dolls, doll carriages, cars, and trucks are the necessary props for these role-playing episodes and should be available to both boys and girls.

The two-year-old child's ability to express her thoughts, feelings, and needs is still limited. However, she is assimilating new words daily and making the transition from the use of phrases to the use of simple and complex sentences. By the end of this year, she will be talking in paragraphs and will be asking an endless stream of questions about everything she encounters.

The child's ability to understand language far surpasses her ability to express herself. She enjoys listening to simple stories describing the adventures of children or animals in childlike roles and requests her favorite book again and again, never seeming to tire of the simple plot and text. She absorbs the words of her favorite story and proudly supplies the last word in a sentence or recites a common refrain.

Although the two-year-old may not recall what she had for lunch today, her ability to remember past events is surprisingly good. Consequently she has a set of expectations based on her previous experiences and is easily upset when events do not conform to her expectations. This "compulsiveness" or rigidity is also seen in her unwillingness to accept a broken cookie (in contrast to just a few short months ago, when any piece of a cookie would do) or a slice of cheese that is missing a corner. This new ability to note discrepancies may be bothersome to adults but represents another important step in the child's cognitive development.

Although the child is more sociable now and enjoys being in the presence of other children, she is not yet ready to participate in cooperative play. She explores peers as if they were inanimate objects, poking and inspecting them. Other two-year-old children may not resist this impersonal scrutiny, but will object strenuously should her exploratory behavior extend to their toys. Children in this age range have just discovered the meaning of the word "mine" and apply it vehemently. It is a rare two-year-old who can share her toys graciously.

## Sit and Spin by Kenner

If you know or have an active, energetic two-year-old child, it is important to find toys to channel her energy into acceptable pursuits, especially during long winter days spent indoors. Sit and Spin by Kenner is a perfect large-muscle toy for indoor use.

This ingenious toy, made out of heavy-duty molded plastic, is virtually indestructible and, best of all, has no motor or batteries to worry about. The child sits on the round base, turns the handle, and generates her own child power to spin as quickly or as slowly as she wishes. She can easily operate this toy by herself, and it is sturdy enough to withstand continued use as she gets older.

## Rhythm Band Set by Creative Playthings

The difference between "making noise" and "making music" is purely academic to the two-year-old child. However you perceive the end result, the child will enjoy the process of "making music" with toy instruments. This delightfully simple activity begins as a natural extension of the "banging" explorations to which all new toys are subjected, but coupled with music, it quickly leads to more sophisticated explorations of rhythm and sound.

Many manufacturers provide separate drums, xylophones, and horns. Purchased individually, the cost of

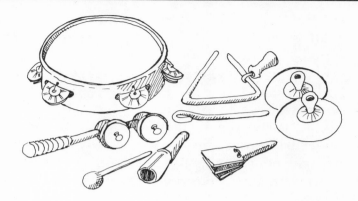

these instruments is generally greater and the quality generally poorer than offered in the Rhythm Band Set by Creative Playthings. This set consists of six well-made percussion instruments: tambourine, cymbals, wood tone block, triangle with striker, wood castanet, and jingle jog. The child will enjoy the variety of sounds offered by this group of instruments. As she gets older, the Rhythm Band Set can be used with friends or incorporated into dramatic play as your child leads her own marching band.

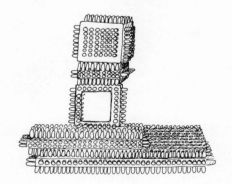

## Bristle Blocks by Playskool

The two-year-old child is not ready to build elaborate structures or representational objects. In fact, she is frustrated by blocks that topple easily, since she does not have the dexterity, know-how, or patience required to carefully balance one wooden block on top of another.

Bristle Blocks by Playskool make building easy and fun for the two-year-old child.

Each block is made out of soft, plastic bristles. With a modest amount of pressure, the bristles interlock and the child is able to pile one block on top of another to create large, free-form sculptures that stay together until she decides to dismantle them. The starter set (#805) contains thirty-two brightly colored blocks in five different shapes. Larger sets containing heads and wheels for constructing people and vehicles are also available but are not necessary for the two-year-old. Like all Playskool building products, Bristle Blocks come in their own sturdy storage container.

## Easy Grip Pegs by Ideal Toy Company

Pegboards are a perfect match for the skills and interests of the two-year-old child. The repetitiousness of the task and the opportunity to practice hand-eye coordination as well as color sorting make it an extremely appealing activity to children in this age range. However, the old-fashioned pegboard set that consisted of slim wooden dowels and a wooden board full of holes is no longer available. It has been removed from the market because young children could easily swallow the narrow pegs. Unfortunately, none of the larger toy manufacturers have developed a safe substitute.

While attempting to find a safe alternative, I discovered Easy Grip Pegs by Ideal Toy Company. These oversized (2½ inches), contoured pegs are easy to grasp, come in four bright colors, and are sold primarily to nursery and public schools. The boards must be purchased separately and come in two sizes, 25 holes and 100 holes. The main drawback to purchasing this set is that the Easy Grip Pegs only come in packages of 100. Although this is a useful amount for a classroom, it is more than is needed at home and also increases the purchase price. However, I still feel that Easy Grip Pegs are worth the investment. To make the cost more competitive with other commercial toys for children in this age range, split the pegs and cost with a friend who also has a two-year-old child or save the extra pegs to give as birthday presents (order two extra boards). It is a gift that will rarely be duplicated and will be greatly appreciated by both the child and her parents.

## Jumbo Wood Beads by Playskool

Stringing beads requires good fine-motor coordination and a long attention span. Not all two-year-old children will enjoy this activity, but for those who are ready, the Playskool Jumbo Wood Beads are an excellent choice. These large, attractive beads come in four colors and four shapes. Two plastic-tipped laces are also included in the set, which comes in its own handy storage container.

For the two-year-old child, stringing beads is a complex undertaking. Carefully knot one end of each lace so that the beads do not fall off as fast as the child puts them on. Also, demonstrate how to hold the bead while inserting the lace through the hole. Once the child masters the necessary sequence, she will enjoy filling each lace with as many beads as it can hold.

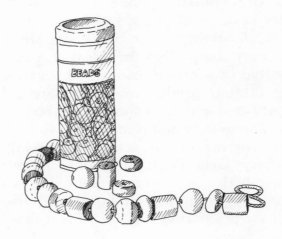

## Dolls

Every child should have at least one doll. Nothing is more natural for a child than imitating the parenting behavior she witnesses each day. For the two-year-old child, the best type of doll is twelve to fifteen inches tall, soft, and washable. There are many excellent dolls on the market, and some can perform feats more elaborate than the average two-year-old could accomplish. I prefer simple baby dolls designed to withstand lots of loving and the unintentional mishandling of any new "parent."

Baby Sofskin (style #2401) by Horseman, shown here, is a moderately priced doll that meets these specifications. She has an appealing face, her eyes open and close, she "drinks" and "wets," and her entire body is made out of soft rubber. This cuddly baby can accompany your child to the bathtub as well as to bed. Horseman has been manufacturing dolls for more than a hundred years and offers a wide selection of dolls which will please any child.

Fisher-Price has recently expanded its toy line to include a family of dolls. Each is approximately thirteen inches, has a soft vinyl face and hands, and is dressed in attractive clothing that fastens easily with Velcro tape (an excellent idea so that even the two-year-old can dress and undress her own baby). The one drawback to these dolls is that their bodies are made out of cloth and therefore discourage the child from bathing her doll.

Childcraft also offers a baby doll with a washable vinyl body who "drinks" and "wets." The unique feature of these eleven-inch baby boy or baby girl dolls is that they are anatomically complete.

No discussion of dolls would be complete without mentioning the Madame Alexander line. These beautifully made dolls have soft vinyl hands, feet, and faces with cloth bodies. My favorites are the Baby Brother and Baby Sister dolls. The features of these two dolls are more similar to a one-year-old than to an infant. They are approximately fifteen inches in height, are beautifully dressed, and cry when moved. The Madame Alexander dolls are known for their high quality but are among the more expensive dolls on the market.

## Doll Carriages

The two-year-old child loves to push a carriage around and is just as pleased with herself whether she is transporting a baby or a collection of blocks. It is hard to find a sturdy, moderately priced doll carriage that resembles the pram the child herself once rode in. The less expensive models are poorly constructed and can barely withstand one accidental crash into a wall or other hard surface. The sturdier versions are priced between sixty and eighty dollars, which is too much from my point of view.

Two excellent compromise models resemble a cross between a carriage and a wagon. Monsanto Learning Products, Inc. offers a simple, open pram made out of heavy-duty molded plastic. The six-inch heavy-duty wheels are fastened securely to the aluminum axles with cotter pins and will not accidentally come loose. This pram, designed for use in a classroom, is sturdy enough to hold a child. A comparably priced, smaller doll's pram is offered by Brio. This model, made out of beechwood and attractively decorated, is imported from Sweden. Both versions, although not exact replicas of the model Mommy uses, will withstand the use and abuse of the young child.

## Construction Trucks by Fisher-Price

For years, the most popular toy trucks for children were miniature metal replicas of the equipment found on construction sites. Recently, Fisher-Price introduced its line of heavy-duty plastic trucks, which are carefully designed to meet the needs of the young child and her parents. The series consists of a dump truck (pictured here), scoop loader, shovel digger, bulldozer, roller grader, and boom crane.

Each large truck is attractively colored in bright yellow and orange and comes with its own removable construction worker. Because the trucks are made of plastic, they are lighter and therefore easier to carry. They have no sharp edges or points, and each truck has large handles, levers, cranks, and scoops that are easily operated by a young child.

A critical feature is that the trucks are rustproof. This is particularly important because toy trucks are commonly used in a sandbox and frequently left outdoors for weeks at a time. You can eaily restore the Fisher-Price trucks to their original state by quickly rinsing them with a garden hose. These trucks are designed to dig, lift, and dump large mounds of earth and will delight girls and boys throughout the ages of two to six years.

## Markers, Crayons, Chalkboard, and Chalk

The two-year-old child enjoys scribbling with pens, pencils, felt-tip markers, and crayons. Her enthusiastic explorations easily extend beyond the edge of her paper, however, so this activity should be supervised.

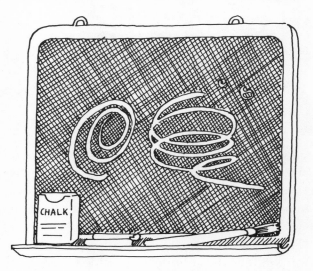

Young children enjoy markers because they require little effort to make lines of vivid colors. However, the child will rarely remember to replace the cap, and so the markers will dry up quickly. For the young artist, inexpensive markers are best. Carter makes broad-tipped, nontoxic, odorless, water-soluble markers that come ten to a package.

Crayons require greater effort to produce bright colors, but they offer shadings that markers lack. Crayola offers good, modestly priced wax crayons that do not bend from the heat of a child's hand. They are nontoxic and come in a variety of sizes. The best size for the two-year-old is the Jumbo Crayola tuck box. These oversized crayons come in eight colors and are easier for the young child to grasp and manipulate.

The least amount of supervision is required when your child is writing on a chalkboard. A two- by three-foot board gives the child ample space to experiment with different colors of chalk. If supplied with a paintbrush and a cup of water, she can also use the board for "water painting." The two-year-old child will not be upset when her "pictures" evaporate. She will happily create new ones.

# VI

# Three to Four Years Old

By age three, a child is a little person capable of a greater range of activities than ever before. A single day bursts with running, climbing, jumping, riding, cutting, pasting, drawing, painting, pretending, talking, listening, looking, and expressing love, hate, joy, and fear. With the endless possibilities, three-year-olds are becoming individuals with strong preferences of their own. Some are budding athletes preferring large-muscle play. Some have long attention spans and sit requesting story after story. Others enjoy creative tasks requiring fine motor manipulations and produce numerous works of art.

Three-year-olds have a number of characteristics in common. Most of them understand the everyday words of adult conversation. Children still differ in their ability to express their thoughts, but by the age of three most can understand the language of simple storybooks. In fact, three-year-olds often delight in the rhyme and rhythm of children's books and, after several repetitions of the story, are able to fill in the last word of a familiar sentence.

Three-year-olds begin to pretend with more imagination and flair than their younger counterparts. They go beyond the earliest pretend telephone conversations and dramatically take on the role of familiar adults in their lives. Being Mommy, Daddy, the bus driver, or the letter carrier becomes common in the play of three-year-olds.

With the prevalence of television, the roles often include "superheroes." Little is required in the way of a costume to inspire a three-year-old to pretend.

Gross motor activities continue to challenge even the quieter, slower-paced three-year-olds. The physical coordination required to ride a tricycle develops during the fourth year, and most children find mastering this skill an exciting process. Riding activities are often an end in themselves but sometimes fit nicely into role playing, as anything that moves can become a fire engine, car, or horse.

As fine motor coordination improves and intellectual ability advances, many activities increase in fun and interest. Creative projects with art materials and toys like puzzles and blocks provide both challenge and satisfaction to three-year-olds. Children exhibit great pride in their accomplishments in such activities. A typical three-year-old might spend a great deal of time setting up an activity, neatly arranging the paper and pencils, and carefully positioning the chair, only to do a five-second scribble and proudly announce, "I've made a boat."

The three-year-old's attempt at making things to represent reality are one step beyond earlier explorations of the materials for their sensual delight. Although adults are often embarrassed to ask what the scribbles "are," the three-year-old is very pleased to exclaim their identity or multiple identities as his fancy changes.

One toy can stimulate many of the described activities simultaneously. For example, a tricycle may provide opportunities for gross motor mastery, the expression of pride in achievement, and role play. And yet as you read this generalized sketch, you may have thought of a number of very different three-year-olds you know who seem to personify one or another of the typical interest areas. Unquestionably each child is unique in temperament and tastes from birth, but these differences crystallize as the child grows and becomes more capable of expressing preferences.

## Tricycles

By age three, your child is ready to make the transition from a four-wheeled riding toy to a tricycle. The ability to pedal rarely emerges before age three, but when it appears it opens new avenues for activity and pleasure. The child can ride around in circles endlessly, simply enjoying the sense of movement, or can pretend that his "vehicle" is the family car, a fire engine or anything else that appeals to his imagination.

Tricycles come in sizes designated by the diameter of the front wheel. The ten-inch size is designed for the average two-year-old child (and not worth the investment). The twelve- to thirteen-inch size would "fit" most three-year-olds and be useful until they are ready to make the transition to a two-wheeler (usually between the ages of five and seven). The best way to choose a tricycle is to have the child mount several in the store. Remember, most seats can be adjusted up or down approximately two inches. The child must be able to get on and off easily and, most important, his feet must reach the pedals. A child riding a tricycle that is too big could

have difficulties balancing and topple over, tricycle and all. Tricycles range in price from nine to thirty dollars. This is not the time to purchase the least expensive model, since a sturdy tricycle will easily last for more than one child.

An excellent reference for more details about safety features and durability of construction is "Tricycles," *Consumer Reports*, vol. 41, no. 11 (November 1976), pp. 623-30.

## Hardwood Blocks by Creative Playthings

Now is the time to purchase one large set of blocks. The three-year-old child wants to make tall towers, sprawling roadways, and elaborate "sculptures." His creations require the use of more blocks than are provided in the smaller, starter sets.

Blocks are one of the best toy investments you can make. They provide opportunities for a child to discover spatial relationships and the relation of parts to the whole. Building requires fine motor coordination and encourages imagination, planning, and problem-solving abilities. A good set of blocks will provide many hours of pleasure for a child from age three on.

The Hardwood Blocks by Creative Playthings consists of fifty-two blocks in nine shapes. They come in a natural hardwood finish, have rounded edges, and are meticulously sanded to provide a smooth surface. The basic block is 1⅜ inches thick, 2¾ inches wide, and 5½ inches long. All of the other blocks are multiples of this size. Although larger sets are available, the pieces offered here will provide the quantity and variety needed to satisfy the young builder.

## Lego Building Sets

The Building Sets by Lego Systems, Inc., are carefully designed for three-year-old children, providing

easily manipulable bricks in a variety of sizes, shapes, and colors, wheels and tires, doors that open and close, windows with movable shutters, and baseplates which act as a foundation for buildings. The basic starter set (Model 110) has 127 pieces. Larger sets include Lego people, which are an attractive feature.

The Lego Building Sets provide opportunities for the child to construct an endless variety of buildings, vehicles, and people. The blocks fit together snugly so that treasured creations cannot be kicked apart unintentionally by a playmate or a parent. In fact, their only drawback is that the connected pieces are occasionally difficult to separate and require an adult's helping hand.

As the child grows, his imagination and skill will grow too. This toy will easily accommodate the demands of the developing child and can be enjoyed alone or with friends.

## The Marble Run by Hancock Associates

This ingenious toy dates back to the early nineteenth century. Some think it was originally designed by the Shakers for their children. The Marble Run consists of zigzagging wooden tracks with roll-through holes. The rhythm, sound, and movement of the marbles making their way from the top of the run to the waiting tray at

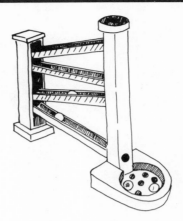

the bottom fascinates the three-year-old child. He enjoys the redundant quality of the activity and quickly discovers the laws of gravity.

Many craftsmen make their own version of a Marble Run. Some versions do not have the handy tray at the bottom. Others vary the size and number of tracks, and some even consist of wooden dowels rather than tracks. A similar toy is also available from Creative Playthings, but it requires that the child construct his own network of ramps and is therefore recommended for five-year-olds. I prefer the sturdy, classic model. This simple toy delights children of all ages and is one that children "rediscover" over and over again.

A note of caution: Marbles are small enough to be swallowed. Most three-year-old children have outgrown the need to put everything in their mouths. If a child is not yet reliable, this toy is not a good choice for him.

## Puzzles

For some three-year-old children, no task is more appealing than putting the scattered pieces of a puzzle correctly in place to form a recognizable picture. They enjoy the process as much as the creation of the product and will quickly disassemble the puzzle and begin over again.

Children in this age range vary in their experience with puzzles, in their ability to concentrate on a task, and in their tolerance for frustration. Puzzles that are too difficult or contain pieces which do not fit together easily can be exasperating. This is one reason why cardboard and rubber puzzles are poor choices for children in this age range. The frames stretch, the pieces bend, and the puzzles become more of a challenge than originally intended.

The inexperienced child should begin with a simple puzzle of five interlocking pieces. Once he masters the concept of putting the pieces together to form the whole, he will quickly graduate to puzzles of increasing complexity. In fact, you should not buy more than two puzzles requiring the same level of skill. The child will not mind doing the same puzzle over and over again, and when he is ready for a new one it should contain at least two additional pieces.

Playskool offers a wide variety of high-quality wooden inlay puzzles consisting of five to twenty interlocking pieces. They are moderately priced, are attractively designed, and will last indefinitely. They depict a broad spectrum of scenes and characters at various levels of complexity (e.g., Sesame Street, Disney, Peanuts, superheroes), and you will easily find one to interest and challenge any child.

## Sewing Boards by Creative Playthings

For the three-year-old child who enjoys tasks that encourage mastery of fine motor skills, Sewing Boards are a good choice. However, this is one toy that requires adult participation. Be prepared to demonstrate the in-and-out pattern of a running stitch more than once. Mastering this skill is not an easy task for a three-year-old; his stitches will be large and haphazard at first.

Many inexpensive cardboard sets are available. Unfortunately, the boards bend and rip easily. The set

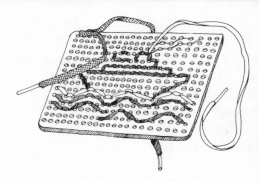

offered by Creative Playthings consists of three firm boards each 7¾ inches by 10¾ inches. Two of the boards have silk-screened designs and the third is blank so that the child can create his own picture or pattern. Sixteen brightly colored sewing laces are also included. This sturdy set will easily withstand repeated use.

## Medical Kit by Fisher-Price

Three-year-olds are miniature adults as they try on many familiar roles in fantasy play. Doctors are commonly admired and imitated by young children as they examine dolls, pets, and parents. "Playing doctor," with realistic-looking medical instruments also may comfort the fears and anxieties of a youngster anticipating a routine checkup or a visit to the hospital.

The Fisher-Price Medical Kit, although expensive, is the best equipped and most durable set I have seen. It

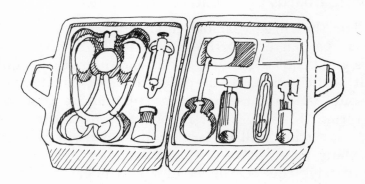

offers several unique features, such as a blood-pressure cuff, a reflex hammer, and an otoscope, as well as the standard equipment such as a stethoscope, needle, thermometer, and pill dispenser. The carrying case is sturdy, easy to open and close, and well designed so that the young physician can put away the tools of his trade. Creative Playthings offers a sophisticated stethoscope (the one item costing approximately half of what this kit costs), but I prefer the variety in the Fisher-Price set.

## Tea Sets

Playing house is a compelling activity for boys and girls. Pretending to be Daddy or Mommy allows three-year-old children to try on the adult roles they are most familiar with and most affected by. Since a significant part of every family's routine is mealtime, children need a sturdy set of dishes to use when playing house.

Children's tea sets come in plastic, china, or aluminum models. Although the bright colors and inexpensive cost of the china and plastic sets make them attractive, they are not good choices. They are easily broken (even a plastic set will crack, especially if stepped on) and they are too small and dainty to be easily manipulated by a three-year-old child. In the long run, you will spend more money replacing broken dishes than if you initially purchase the more expensive but sturdier aluminum set.

The Tea Set by Creative Playthings is a seventeen-piece set made out of heavy-gauge aluminum. It contains service for four (cups, saucers, and plates), a covered teapot, a covered sugar bowl, and a creamer. The cups and plates are large enough so that a pretend "party" can easily convert into a real meal or snack time. Creative Playthings also offers a set of knives, forks, and spoons (service for four), pots and pans, and a baking set. All are realistically styled and sturdily constructed from heavy-gauge aluminum.

## Hats by Childcraft

Unlike the two-year-old child, who needs no trappings to pretend, the three-year-old child wants to wear something that represents the role he is assuming. The simple addition of a tie, a cape, a pocketbook, or a hat makes him feel "dressed" and enables him to be that other person.

The set of six hats offered by Childcraft are excellent toys for a three-year-old child. They are made of heavy-gauge molded plastic and consist of a helmet with goggles, a cowboy hat, a construction worker's helmet, a fire-fighter's hat, a "straw" hat, and a derby. Moderately priced, these hats provide a child with easy access to a wide variety of roles.

## Arts and Crafts Materials

### Scissors

Cutting, like bicycle riding, is an activity preschoolers enjoy practicing over and over again. However, nothing is more disheartening for a child than practicing a new skill with a tool that minimizes his chances for success. A child's scissors must be designed specifically for his use. Adult scissors are too sharp and too large for a child to manipulate effectively. Poorly constructed metal and plastic scissors are too flimsy and the blades too dull to

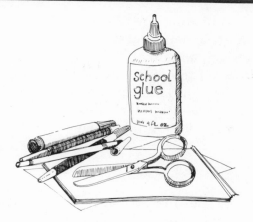

cut even the thinnest piece of paper. The coordination required for cutting is difficult enough for the three-year-old child to master without his being impeded by poorly constructed scissors.

Good scissors can be purchased for less than one dollar. Stores that carry school supplies usually have an excellent selection (for example, scissors by Ja-son). A four-inch pair of scissors is the best size for the preschooler. The edges should be blunt and the blades sharp enough to cut materials easily. Some scissors have handles covered with a heavy vinyl coating. This makes it easier to grip and less tiring for the beginner to use.

Note: Left-handed children should not use scissors designed for right-handed children. Most stores carry scissors specially designed for lefties. If the child you are shopping for is left-handed, be sure to request the correct scissors.

## Paper

Children use paper faster than adults use stamps. A ten-minute painting session may easily result in five works of "art." With all the other uses a child will find for a pad of paper, the cost of keeping him adequately supplied will mount quickly. The best place to purchase drawing paper is from a large school-supplies store. A ream (500 sheets) of nine- by twelve-inch drawing paper will cost less than a penny a sheet. (At J. L. Hammett Company in Boston, a ream of lightweight drawing paper is $3.70; a ream of medium-weight drawing paper is $4.20.) Buying paper in large quantities is not only more economical but prevents tear-filled scenes when the child's one and only pad of unlined paper cannot be found.

## Paints

Painting can be messy, but it is also fun and instructional for the three-year-old child. The haphazard mixing of colors results in exciting discoveries of different tints, shades, and hues. The most common type of watercolor sets consists of six or more pads of paint and a small paintbrush neatly packaged in its own plastic tray. Unfortunately, the colors that result from their use are pale and disappointing to the young artist. In addition, most children forget to wash their brushes before switching from one color to the next, and the closely spaced pads of paint quickly blend into a nondescript muddy brown.

The best paint set for a child is an inexpensive set of small bottles of fluorescent watercolors distributed by Sanford. The set consists of six ¾-ounce bottles of vibrant colors, already mixed and ready to use. The paints are water-soluble and nontoxic. The separate bottles make it easier to avoid unintentional color blending. You can open one bottle of paint at a time for the child or place separate brushes in each bottle. The lids close tight and the paints do not dry up or flake.

## Glue

Glue is better than paste because it is easier to spread and does not flake when it dries. Elmer's Glue, one of the more readily available brand-name products, is perfect for children. It is nontoxic, comes in a plastic container, and washes off hands and clothing easily. Elmer's Glue dries quickly and works equally well with paper, wood, and cloth. It can be purchased in varying quantities (from 1¼ ounces to one gallon) and will last indefinitely if the container is closed when not in use.

# VII

# Four to Five Years Old

The four-year-old child is a delightful mixture of dramatic contradictions. One minute she is planning her social calendar and the next minute she is whining to be carried. One minute she is grappling with complicated issues ("Is Santa Claus real?"; "When I get big, do you get little?") and the next minute she is babbling in "baby talk." One minute she is sunshine and giggles and the next minute she is the picture of complete despair.

The year from the fourth to the fifth birthday is a time of important transitions. The four-year-old child is ready to take the first step beyond the family constellation. Friendships emerge in importance, and preferences about playmates are strong and definite. Passions run high in this fifth year of life, and a best friend can become a hated enemy over a small slight. Four-year-olds can quickly come to blows over disputes about property or turns. At other times, however, they are the picture of cooperation. Learning to share, taking turns, and losing as well as winning are all critical elements in the socialization process that is occurring during this year. As she masters social skills as well as integrates the many cognitive and manipulative skills she has been practicing, the child begins to enjoy board games and other competitive activities.

The four-year-old child is an agile climber, a fast runner, and a budding gymnast. Doing things better, swinging higher, or going faster than others suddenly becomes important to her. She is more daring than ever before and uses her gross motor skills to exhibit her new-found sense of competence. She climbs to the top of the jungle gym, pumps when on a swing, and loves the sensation of speed as she cascades down a hill on her Big Wheels.

The four-year-old child's sense of humor is often hard for adults to appreciate, but her goodwill and hilarity are infectious. The jokes ("You know what?" "What?" "That's what!"), the bathroom humor, and the sense of the ridiculous blossom. She rediscovers many of her picture books and appreciates the humor and absurdities that she did not understand in her earlier years. The child continues to enjoy stories and can listen to longer tales and follow more complicated plots. She also enjoys "playing" with language as she rhymes words, makes up songs, and weaves her own tall tales.

The four-year-old also works quietly for long periods of time on important projects. Her attention span is longer and her ability to plan and carry out multistepped activities has expanded. She will build complicated and realistic structures that become the setting for dramatic play. She is no longer satisfied with imitations. She wants tools that really hammer and saw, a camera that takes *real* pictures, and a record player that plays *real* records. She feels "grown up," and the projects she envisions require real tools.

This growing sense of competence and independence often results in behaviors that are similar to the testing of the two-year-old child and the rebellion of the adolescent. Experimenting with "swearing," crossing a street without permission, and refusing to wear a jacket on a cold day are all part of the four-year-old child's struggle to find out how separate and independent she really is from her parents. Recognizing the child's "maturity" is important, but maintaining the balance between the few things she can do independently and the many things that still require supervision is a critical task for parents and other care givers during this year of transition.

This is the last of the preschool years. Recommending effective and enjoyable toys is a harder task as each child's interests and tastes diverge. You should observe the child's play and give some thought to the skills you would like to encourage. By the end of this year, selecting toys is a collaborative effort between what the child requests and what you think is worthwhile. Peer pressures grow, and children want whatever their friends have. You must distinguish between toys that will have lasting appeal to the child and requests that are the product of momentary whims. Also, be careful to discern when requests are influenced by advertisements that work cleverly to make children their customers.

## Three Ladder Swing Set by Child Life Play Specialties

Swinging and climbing are favorite pastimes for children of all ages, and there is no better equipment on which to practice these skills than the swing sets offered

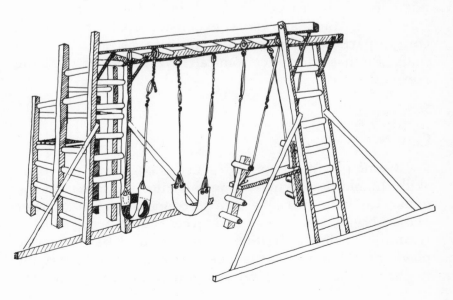

by Child Life. Each set is carefully and sturdily designed to withstand years of energetic use. They are made of durable wood that blends attractively into any outdoor environment and never rusts. Design features such as ¼-inch nuts that fit flat against the wood, eliminating the hazard of scrapes and scratches from protruding nuts and bolts, and nonslip ladder rung surfaces are examples of the planning and quality incorporated into each set.

The Three Ladder Swing Set is the basic unit. It consists of a swing, a horse that holds two children, and a trapeze bar. All three are carefully spaced for safety, and children can raise or lower each swing or rearrange their order as their fancy dictates. The frame consists of three climbing ladders. The lower rungs on each of the side ladders are more closely spaced to encourage the young climber. More elaborate sets and additional accessories are also available. The Jungle End Swing Set (illustrated here) combines the basic unit with a climbing gym. Slides, climbing ropes, and four-unit swing sets can also be purchased. Child Life also offers an excellent toddler swing (see illustration) made of flexible rubber belting attached in such a way that a little child will not tumble out even if she forgets to hold on. Although the Child Life Swing Sets are more expensive than their metal counterparts, their durability and safe, attractive design make them a more economical investment in the long run.

## Games

Game playing requires the use of cognitive and social skills. In addition to mastering the rules and moves of the game, the child must be able to cooperate with another person, wait her turn, and accept losing as well as winning. Losing is frequently the hardest part of game playing for children in this age range, and a child may try to change the rules, "cheat," or quit rather than lose. It is only through experience that she learns to be a gracious loser as well as a gracious winner.

The most suitable games for children of this age require no reading skills. The simplest beginner board games involve color-matching tasks. Two excellent examples are Candyland and Winnie the Pooh.

Candyland by Milton Bradley, a simple game designed for two to four players, continues to be a favorite of young children. A player draws a card from the deck and moves her playing piece to the corresponding color square on the game board. The goal is to be the first to arrive at the gingerbread house.

In Winnie the Pooh by Walt Disney, a player selects a colored disc from a grab bag and moves her playing piece to the corresponding square on the game board. The first to reach the pot of honey is the winner.

Two other games that capitalize on the young child's interest in constructing products are Snoopy's Dog House and Blockhead.

The goal of Snoopy's Dog House by Playskool is to be the first player to construct a doghouse for Snoopy. Each player spins the dial and takes the piece of the doghouse indicated by the pointer (e.g., wall, roof). This game can be played by two to four participants.

Blockhead by Chopper demands that the child anticipate the consequences of her actions. Each player selects one of the brightly colored, irregularly shaped blocks and adds it to a structure being constructed. The first player to precipitate the downfall of the structure loses. This game can be played alone or with others and is enjoyed by children of varying ages.

Once the child can consistently recognize numbers, card games and dominoes are excellent choices. Any handy deck of cards will do for a game of Go Fish or War. The best set of dominoes for children in this age range is an inexpensive 28-piece wooden set offered by Milton Bradley. Although instructions are given for complex variations of this game, a simple version is best for the four-year-old: Each player selects seven tiles from the "pool." Alternating turns, a player must match one of her tiles to the unattached end of the playing tiles.

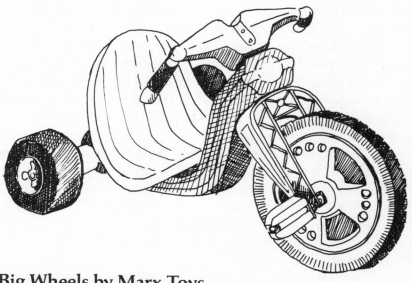

## Big Wheels by Marx Toys

You know spring has arrived when you hear the loud rumble of Big Wheels. These low-slung, hollow tricycles are perfect for the four-year-old child. They go faster than ordinary tricycles, maneuver easily, and negotiate sharp turns without tipping. Big Wheels allow the child to experience an exhilarating sense of control and mastery over her vehicle.

Although this tricycle is suggested by the manufacturer for children between three* and seven years of age, many three-year-olds are not tall enough to reach the pedals, which are located on the front wheel. By age four, children are able to assume this unorthodox riding position with ease. Big Wheels come in a variety of colors

---

*A smaller version, called Mini Wheels, is also available. Unfortunately, it is sized primarily for the two-year-old (who uses it in the same manner she would use any four-wheeled riding toy) and is too small for most three-year-old children.

and styles, but all are constructed in the same durable manner. Fortunately, the seat can be adjusted to allow for growth, since the child will still enjoy riding her Big Wheels when she is six and seven years of age.

## Hot Bat by Lil Slugger

Mastering throwing, catching, and hitting a ball is as time-consuming for the four-year-old as mastering walking was for the one-year-old. Children enjoy practicing new skills again and again but need the cooperation of tools that allow them to succeed. Hot Bat makes it possible for the novice batter to experience the thrill of hitting a "home run." The stubby, extra-wide bat with a narrow handle and the hollow plastic ball are appropriately designed to meet the needs and abilities of the preschooler. The lightweight plastic bat is easy to swing, and the wide surface area makes it possible to "get a hit" if the pitcher can get the ball over the plate. Children of all ages enjoy playing ball with the Hot Bat.

## Camera by Banner

This inexpensive (less than three dollars) plastic camera (style number W 20 A) looks just like a grown-up's camera and takes real pictures. It comes with a lens cap and carrying strap and takes sixteen color or black-and-white photographs with each roll of 120 film. The camera is equipped with three distance ranges and three apertures for varying weather conditions. The child looks through the viewfinder and snaps away. Now she just has to have the patience to wait until the pictures are developed.

## Handy Andy Tool Set by Skil Craft Corp.

Tools can be used in dramatic play (e.g., pretending to be a fix-it person), but most frequently, the four-year-old child wants to use her tools to construct boats, houses, furniture for dolls, and works of art. Plastic tool sets, although recommended by most manufacturers for children age three and older, do not meet the needs of a child in this age range.

Skil Craft offers a range of inexpensive (from five to seven dollars), sturdy tools scaled in size for use by a child. The Handy Andy sets contain a hammer, pliers, a screwdriver, a handsaw, and a ruler. Some sets also include a steel triangle and sandpaper and come in plastic or metal carrying cases. These sets are designed to be used for cutting and pounding, so the tools have functional sharp points and/or edges. Children should be shown how to use tools carefully, and adult supervision is recommended when a child undertakes a project. Supplied with wood, nails, and a good tool set, a child can create her own unique set of treasured playthings.

## Lincoln Logs, Scout Set, by Playskool

As the four-year-old child tries to build more complex and realistic structures, she will delight in the use of Lincoln Logs. These nontoxic wooden logs enable a child to build realistic cabins, houses, forts, fences, and bridges. The interlocking pieces create secure structures that can become part of ongoing fantasy play with miniature people and animals.

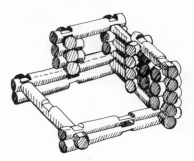

The Scout Set contains 90 pieces: full logs (1½", 4½", 7½", 10½"), split logs (10½"), roof boards (12"), large gables, and a chimney. A smaller Pioneer Set (74 pieces) and four larger sets (ranging from 128 to 430 pieces) are also available. The quantity and price of the Scout Set make it the best initial investment in this building system. All pieces are interchangeable, and each set comes in its own sturdy container, making storage easy and neat.

## Playtiles by Playskool

This advanced version of a pegboard enables the four-year-old child to create beautiful mosaic designs and pictures. No matter how random the pattern, the end result is impressive. The child will experience a sense of accomplishment when she fills the entire board with tiles and will be proud of the product she creates.

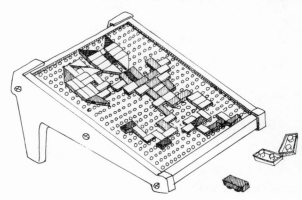

Playtiles contain 224 square, rectangular, and triangular tiles in four colors. They are easy to manipulate and snap securely into the board, but the tiles are small and scatter easily. Once they are removed from their original package, it is wise to store the tiles in a plastic container.

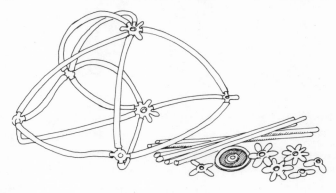

## Construct-O-Straws by Parker Brothers

This moderately priced, delightful toy adds a new dimension to building. Each set contains an assortment of brightly colored polyethylene straws that bend, curve, and can be cut to different lengths. It also contains *connectors* to hold the straws together, *stiffeners* to make the straws rigid, and *wheels* that enable the child's products to move.

Children in this age range are intrigued by the endless possibilities of the bendable straws. A child's creations may range from lovely flowers to complex configurations resembling molecular models. The straws are attractive, are easy to work with, and can be used over and over again.

## Etch-a-Sketch by Ohio Art

This unique toy has been amusing children for years. The magical quality of lines that appear with the flick of a dial and move up or down, right or left, or in circles

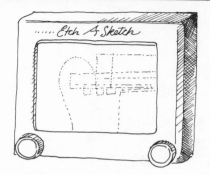

delights the four-year-old child. With this toy, a child can create representational pictures or complex geometric patterns. It is also fun to use with a friend.

Etch-a-Sketch is a five- by seven-inch screen encased in a sturdy plastic frame. The magic lines are made from nontoxic aluminum powder. There are two dials on the frame: One makes the lines progress vertically; the other makes the lines progress horizontally; and if you turn both knobs at once, curves appear. Etch-a-Sketch is the perfect companion for the four-year-old child during periods of confinement, when she is traveling, or when she is in bed with a cold.

## Play Mobile System by Schaper

This modern-day version of previous generations' toy soldiers offers a variety of figures in different settings: cavalry, Indians, knights in shining armor, construction workers, medical teams, and fire fighters. Each set contains sturdy plastic figures, three inches high, and appropriate accessories, from horses to eating utensils. The figures' heads, arms, and legs move and they can sit, stand, ride a horse, or hold a tool. The figures and accessories are attractively designed and easy to manipulate. My one criticism of this toy system is that female figures are rarely included. Unfortunately, in the few instances when they do appear, it is in stereotypic roles such as "nurse."

The four-year-old child delights in arranging and acting out the various scenarios represented by the figures. The Play Mobile Systems come in a variety of sizes ranging from starter sets of 22 pieces to deluxe sets of more than 100 pieces. It is easy to get carried away when purchasing these attractive toys. However, the figures and accessories are interchangeable, and several starter sets rather than one deluxe set will provide a child with greater variety for less cost.

## Phonographs

Selecting a record player for a young child is not an easy task. The more commonly available, moderately priced, portable record players are not sturdy enough to withstand the manipulations of a four-year-old child. The cases are made out of cardboard and the arms and needles are easily dislodged.

Fisher-Price offers a Music Box Record Player (recommended for children between two and six years of age) that comes with its own set of records and requires no batteries or electricity. It has a knob that winds up the turntable, and the nubs in the record grooves activate the music box. It is sturdy and easy for the young child to carry and manipulate, but it is quickly outgrown as the child's taste in music expands beyond the ten tunes provided on the records.

Obitron offers a unique phonograph (Model OB 885) for children that is safe, indestructible, and attractive. It is made out of heavy-duty plastic and is battery-operated. The child puts the record on the turntable, closes the lid, and listens to her favorite song. There are no electrical outlets to be concerned about, no arms and needles to be replaced, and no scratched records. This compact phonograph plays both 33⅓ and 45 rpm records and is moderately priced. (Kenner offers a similar phonograph but, unfortunately, it only plays 45 rpm records. Most children's records are 33⅓ rpm.)

## Records

Children's records vary dramatically in content and quality. Unfortunately, the best records are rarely found in local stores. The easiest way to purchase good records for a child is to order them through catalogues. Three excellent sources are as follows:

> Children's Music and Book Catalogue
> 1201-C East Ball Road
> Anaheim, CA 92805

> Children's Book and Music Center
> 5373 W. Pico Blvd.
> Los Angeles, CA 90019

> The Children's Center
> 3 Maryvale Lane
> Peabody, MA 01960

Among my favorite selections for children are the albums *And One and Two* and *Ella Jenkins*, both by Folkway Records. Ella Jenkins, known for her contributions to the teaching of folk music and rhythmic activities to children, involves her audience in a delightful musical experience.

Three Hap Palmer Records by Educational Activities, Inc.—*Learning Basic Skills Through Music; Creative Movement and Rhythmic Exploration;* and *Simplified Folk Songs*—are fun, even though the album titles sound formal. The catchy tunes (e.g., "Marching Around the Alphabet") are quickly mimicked by the preschooler.

Weston Wood Studios have recorded the best in children's literature and offer book/record combinations at a modest price. Children delight in listening to these well-read stories while looking at the pictures in their own books.

In *Mother Goose* by Caedmon Records, the nursery tales, performed by Cyril Ritchard, Celeste Holm, and Boris Karloff, will hold the attention of adults as well as children.

The popular television program "Sesame Street" has spawned many entertaining records for young children. *Havin' Fun with Ernie and Bert* by Columbia Records invites your child to participate in the musical escapades of two of the show's characters.

The catchy, thought-provoking songs on *Free to Be You and Me* by Bell Records are fun to listen to and sing. Songs such as "William's Doll" and "Parents Are People" are two excellent examples of this ambitious undertaking by Marlo Thomas and her very talented friends.

# VIII

# Alternative Toys: Household Objects and Homemade Toys

With a little imagination, the contents of a home can have as much play value as the contents of a well-stocked toy store. The child delights in exploring drawers and cabinets, is fascinated by the working of kitchen utensils, and easily converts canned foods into building blocks and pot lids into cymbals. The unhampered mind of the young child generates many original uses for household objects. In addition, common household supplies can be used to construct more traditional toys such as mobiles, shape sorters, and beads for stringing.

Constructing the homemade toys described in this chapter requires no special skills or talents. They are easy to make and can be as simple or as elaborate as your skill and tastes dictate. Many of the toys will be constructed out of cardboard and thus will not be as sturdy as commercially made wooden or plastic versions. However, some toys have only a short life span in the interest spectrum of a child, and the less durable homemade plaything can adequately fulfill the toy need.

Many adults derive pleasure from watching a child play with a toy they have made for him. However, they must be prepared to see the toy they have worked so diligently to make used incorrectly or handled roughly by the child. For those parents who do not have the time nor the inclination to make toys, this chapter contains age-appropriate suggestions for the use of everyday supplies in various activities such as arts and crafts, fantasy play, and cooking.

The safety guidelines outlined earlier apply to all playthings whether they are purchased, homemade, or only a collection of common household objects. Playthings should be screened to ensure that:

- no toy or piece of a toy is smaller than 1¼ inches in diameter and 2¼ inches in depth
- there are no small parts that may fall off and be swallowed or inhaled
- there are no sharp edges or points that can cut, poke, or pinch a child
- all paints and dyes are nontoxic
- broken or damaged items are removed

## Birth to Crawling

### Mobile

Providing something interesting for a newborn to look at is not difficult. Using the information experts have provided about the skills and interests of the newborn, you can construct a satisfactory mobile with a few simple supplies. For example, experts tell us that babies are most attracted to images of the human face. Also, they tend to look to their right side most of the time and see best when items are between five and eighteen inches from their face. All of these features have been incorporated into a simple mobile constructed from a coat hanger, string, markers, and poster board.

Unfortunately, I know of no easy, inexpensive way to construct a musical, revolving mobile. The mobile described here, however, is light enough to move with the slightest breeze. A note of caution: Mobiles are only for *looking at*. When a baby is three to four months of age and begins reaching for objects, he is ready for the sturdier crib gym.

*Materials*
wire coat hanger
kite string
white poster board
markers
yarn
plant hook

*Procedure*

1. Wrap the yarn around the surface of the coat hanger.
2. Draw three circles, each four inches in diameter, on the poster board and cut them out.
3. Draw a face on each circle with markers.
4. Poke a small hole in the middle of each face.
5. Cut three pieces of kite string, each approximately ten inches long.
6. Insert a string through the small hole in the center of the face and knot it. Tie the other end to the coat hanger. Repeat for each face.
7. Insert the plant hook into the ceiling so that the mobile will be correctly positioned over the right side of the crib.
8. Hang the mobile from the plant hook with the kite string. Make sure that the faces are hanging twelve to fourteen inches from the surface of the mattress.

## Crib Gym

At around three months of age a baby begins to use his hands to explore interesting objects. Although his motions appear random at first, reaching and grasping may be encouraged with a simple crib gym. (This is definitely the time to remove the mobile, which is too fragile to withstand the batting and tugging of the three-to seven-month-old child.) The baby's actions should be rewarded with movement or sounds. Brightly colored objects that are easy to grasp are most appropriate.

*Materials*
cardboard tube (from
    aluminum foil roll)
sewing elastic
contact paper
objects to hang from crib
    gym: measuring spoons,
    plastic bracelets, rattle

*Procedure*
1. Cover the cardboard tube with contact paper.
2. Attach objects to pieces of elastic. (It is better to use elastic than string since it is more flexible and will expand with the baby's tugs, giving the entire gym more bounce.) Be sure the objects you choose have holes so they can be attached. Insert the elastic through the hole and sew or knot the elastic. Then, leaving approximately two inches of elastic hanging down, wrap the rest of the elastic around the cylinder and again sew or knot the ends together. Repeat this procedure for each object to be hung from the gym.
3. Cut a piece of elastic that is the width of the crib plus six inches.
4  Insert this elastic through the cylinder, leaving approximately three inches hanging from each side.
5. Attach each end to the side of the crib. Tie it rather than stitch it so that you can remove the gym easily for naps and at bedtime.

## One Year to Eighteen Months Old

Once a baby masters crawling, his play environment extends beyond the boundaries of his crib to his home. Exploration means tasting, touching, and throwing objects. This is the age when children delight in emptying the contents of a drawer, cabinet, or container. The one-year-old delights in repetitive actions, and considers even the most commonplace item a fascinating toy.

## Collectibles

A container full of objects will provide the opportunity for two of the favorite pastimes of the one-year-old child: dumping and exploring objects. Select items that are dispensable and easy to wash. Exploration means mouthing, so it helps if the objects can be rinsed off frequently.

*Materials*

two one-gallon containers with lids (e.g., clean, empty ice-cream containers)

collection of household items: toothbrush, measuring spoons, measuring cups, honey dipper, spoon, empty thread spools, corn butterer (an inexpensive plastic device for buttering corn on the cob, with an opening and closing mechanism that delights children in this age range), etc.

*Procedure*

1. Open and close container lid several times so that it loosens up enough for a child to manipulate it.
2. Provide an extra container so that the baby can transfer the objects from one container to another.
3. Decorate the containers with contact paper. (If you

wish, use two different solid colors so that you can informally begin to teach color labels—e.g., "Put everything back into the yellow container now.")
4. Put collection of objects into the container.

## First Book

Your baby's first book must be sturdy, should depict familiar objects in bold, clear pictures, should be easy to carry and easy to manipulate. A homemade first book is easy to construct and can be tailored to the interest of the individual baby in a way that a purchased book cannot. Select pictures that are most likely to interest the baby now and add to the book as he is ready to learn new words.

*Materials*
old magazines
poster board
glue
hole puncher
hole reinforcers
three metal loose-leaf
   rings

*Procedure*
1. Cut out pictures from magazines—e.g., cup, spoon, dog, cat, baby, man, woman, house, car, truck, tree, flower.
2. Cut out rectangles approximately 8 by 11 inches from the poster board.
3. Paste one picture on each side of the rectangles, leaving a one-inch margin all around the picture. (The edges will be abused from carrying and turning the pages. The border ensures that the pictures won't rip as easily or as quickly.)
4. Punch three holes in each page, making sure to line up each with the other (a good spacing is 1¼ inches from

the top, 1¼ inches from the bottom, and in the middle).
5. Paste reinforcers around each hole on both sides.
6. Insert rings.

## Shape Sorter

A child's first shape sorter should not be complex. Discriminating between two distinct shapes is challenging for the one-year-old. This task requires the ability to concentrate, a tolerance for frustration when the objects do not go into the holes immediately, and the ability to discriminate between the shapes. These are all sophisticated skills for the twelve- to eighteen-month-old. (Note: when you construct your shape sorter, make sure that the round object cannot be inserted in the square hole or vice versa.)

*Materials*
an empty two-pound
  coffee can with lid
contact paper
three empty spools of
  thread
three empty pocket-sized
  matchboxes
sharp scissors or single-
  edge razor blade

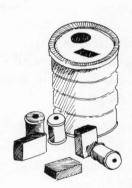

*Procedure*
1. Cover the matchboxes with contact paper so that they look like little blocks. Leave the spools plain.
2. Trace the outline of the narrow side of the matchbox on the plastic coffee can lid.
3. Trace the outline of the base of the spool on the lid. Leave two inches between the two shapes.
4. With sharp scissors or a single-edge razor blade, cut

out the shapes, making the openings slightly larger than the outlines.

5. Cover the can with contact paper.

## Eighteen Months to Two Years Old

Exploring objects and practicing simple skills are still the dominate mode of behavior for children in this age range. The following activities offer ample opportunities for both of these interests.

## Modeling Dough

The eighteen-month-old child is not interested in "making" shapes, but he will enjoy fingering, squeezing, smelling, rolling, and pinching the dough.(By age two, he will enjoy using rolling pins, cookie cutters, and dull knives for cutting while working with the dough.) Homemade dough is easier to work with, softer, and lasts longer than commercially available products. (To store the dough, wrap it tightly in plastic wrap, place it in a plastic bag, and store it in a closet or the refrigerator.) Also, if the child has an irresistible urge to taste the dough, you'll know exactly what he is putting in his mouth.

*Materials*

2 cups flour
2 cups cold water
1 cup salt
2 tablespoons oil

4 teaspoons cream of
 tartar
food coloring

*Procedure*

1. Pour all ingredients into a two-quart pot and stir over medium-high heat until the flour mixture leaves the sides of the pan.
2. Divide the dough into three parts. Add two drops of a different food coloring to each part and mix.
3. Let dough cool for about ten minutes before handling.

# Puzzle

Each piece of a child's first puzzle should depict a distinct object rather than be a fragment of a picture. Children vary in the strategies they employ when presented with a puzzle. Some children move a piece from opening to opening until it slides in easily. Other children examine the spaces visually before making an attempt to place the piece in the correct opening. Hand-eye coordination and shape discrimination are two important skills a child uses in mastering a puzzle.

*Materials*
cardboard carton
three cookie cutters with
distinct shapes and easy-
to-grasp handles (e.g.,
star, half-moon,
diamond)
sharp scissors or single-
edge razor blade
glue
contact paper in a solid
color

*Procedure*
1. Cut three flaps off the carton and trim them all to six by fourteen inches.
2. Trace the outline of the three shapes onto two of the pieces of cardboard, being careful to leave at least one inch between each shape. Also line up each shape exactly on both flaps.
3. Cut out the shapes on each flap, making the outline slightly larger than the tracing.
4. Glue the three pieces of cardboard together, using the solid flap as the bottom piece and carefully lining up the other two pieces.
5. Cover the sides, bottom, and top of the puzzle board with solid-color contact paper (a pattern will be

distracting for a child trying to concentrate on the discrimination task). Carefully cut away the paper from the area within the shapes.
6. Insert the cookie cutters into their matching cutouts.

## Two to Three Years Old

The toddler is still more interested in how things feel than in what he can construct. Although his fine motor coordination is better than that of younger children, his attention span is brief. He will frequently spend more time gathering the necessary materials for an activity than actually using them.

### Water Play

Children enjoy the sensations of warm water cascading through their fingers and can be content pouring water from one container to another. No formal equipment is needed for water play. The kitchen sink is usually the best location because it is deeper than other sinks. Pull a sturdy chair over to the sink, let the child stand on it, put several unbreakable cups, spoons, and other utensils into the sink, turn on warm water, and he is all set. Sometimes I fill the sink with several inches of water rather than let the water continue to run. The child will probably have different preferences on different days. I do not recommend putting soapsuds in the water. Although a child may enjoy the way they look and feel, most two-year-olds find it hard to resist pouring themselves a drink, and sudsy water is obviously not the best liquid to be ingested. (Don't forget to pull up the child's sleeves and put an apron on him. He will get wet!)

*Materials*

| | |
|---|---|
| sink | cups, spoons, plates, |
| water | colander, hand beater, |
| chair | etc.—all unbreakable |
| plastic apron | squirt bottle |

## Pasting

This is the time to save scraps of material, Styrofoam package fillers, magazines, colored paper, and other materials for pasting. Collages offer the child an opportunity to explore the properties of glue in conjunction with different materials.

Glue is generally easier to use than paste because it is easier to spread. The best procedure to facilitate gluing for the young child is to pour a small amount of glue into a paper cup or the top of a plastic container. (If you use a paper cup, you may want to cut the sides to a height of 1½ inches to make it easier for the child to reach into.) Many two-year-old children do not like to get their hands messy. If this is the case with the child you're working with, provide a cotton swab for spreading the glue. You may have to demonstrate the process (spreading the glue, pressing the scrap on the glued spot) once or twice, but then step back. He will want to do it himself!

*Materials*

glue (e.g., Elmer's)　　　　scraps (magazine pictures,
paper cup　　　　　　　　　 fabric, buttons, Stryo-
cotton swab　　　　　　　　 foam, packing fillers)
paper, cardboard

*Procedure*
1. Spread a plastic tablecloth over the worktable.
2. Provide an interesting selection of scraps to be glued.
3. Provide a small amount of glue and a cotton swab for spreading the glue.
4. Provide paper or cardboard as a backing.

## Spool Stringing

Mastery of fine motor skills intrigues many children. Spool stringing is an activity that can be repeated over and over again. In addition to the delight in the process, the child has the reward of making a necklace that he can wear.

*Materials*

24-inch shoelace with
    plastic tip
empty thread spools (at
    least ten, depending on
    their size)

*Procedure*

1. Knot one end of the shoelace.
2. Demonstrate to the child how to hold the spool, which end of the shoelace to insert, and how to pull the spool down to the knotted end once it is on the string.

## Three to Four Years Old

Children in this age range delight in simple tasks that result in a product. Baking, gluing, and sewing cards are three activities that allow a child to practice skills while making things he can share with the rest of the family.

## Gluing

The three-year-old child is ready for more elaborate gluing activities than the two-year-old. In addition to using scraps, different macaroni shapes make interesting products for children in this age range. Elbows, shells, and bows can be painted after being glued. A drop of food coloring in the glue adds an interesting dimension to the process as well as providing an attractive background for the shells.

*Materials*

selection of scraps or
    macaroni
glue
food coloring

paper cup
cotton swab
paper
paint

*Procedure*
1. Cover the working surface with a plastic tablecloth.
2. Provide an interesting selection of macaroni.
3. Put a small amount of glue in a paper cup, add a drop of food coloring, and mix.
4. Provide a cotton swab if the child is reluctant to spread glue with his finger.
5. Provide a piece of paper.
6. Provide paint should he want to paint the shells after gluing them.

## Baking Sugar Cookies

Baking is a particularly intriguing activity. Mixing ingredients together and observing the transition from one consistency and color to another fascinate a child, and, best of all, the end result is edible. Learning to crack eggshells and to measure and mix ingredients together make him feel grown up. Chocolate-chip cookies are easy to make (the recipe can be found on the package of chocolate chips) and are delicious to eat. Sugar cookies require more patience, since the dough must be refrigerated before being rolled, but being able to cut out shapes makes the waiting worthwhile for most children.

*Materials*

2/3  cup shortening
¾   cup sugar
½   teaspoon vanilla
1    egg
4    teaspoons milk

2   cups sifted all-purpose flour
1½ teaspoons baking powder
¼   teaspoon salt

*Procedures*
1. Preheat oven to 375°.
2. Thoroughly cream shortening, sugar, and vanilla.
3. Add egg; beat till light and fluffy.
4. Stir in milk.

5. Sift together dry ingredients; blend into creamed mixture.
6. Divide dough in half.
7. Chill one hour.
8. On lightly floured surface, roll dough to ⅛ inch.
9. Cut desired shapes with cutters.
10. Bake on greased cookie sheet at 375° about six to eight minutes.
11. Cool slightly; remove from sheet.
12. Cool on rack. Makes 2 dozen.

## Stringing Macaroni

Making simple products that can be worn or eaten are fun. Rigatoni noodles are perfect for stringing. Although they will crack if stepped on, they are strong enough to withstand normal manipulation. They can be painted and then strung on a shoelace to make an attractive necklace.

*Materials*
uncooked rigatoni noodles     24-inch shoelace with
paint                              plastic tip

*Procedure*
1. Cover the working surface with a plastic tablecloth.
2. Let the child paint the rigatoni noodles with water-color paints.
3. When they are dry, knot the end of the shoelace.
4. Let the child string the noodles.

## Sewing Cards

Sewing cards are enjoyed by the child who has a long attention span and good hand-eye coordination. The motion of going in and out of the holes in a running stitch pattern is often difficult for a child in this age range. Be prepared to demonstrate the stitch more than once. Note:

The twelve-inch length of shoelace is easiest for a child in this age range to manipulate. A longer string will get tangled and complicate the activity needlessly.

*Materials*
poster board
black marker
hole puncher
12-inch shoelaces of
    different colors

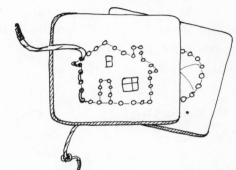

*Procedure*
1. Cut out rectangles approximately 8 by 11 inches from the poster board.
2. Draw a simple outline of familiar objects, such as a house, boat, snowman, and tree.
3. Knot one end of a shoelace.
4. Punch holes in the picture, following the outline you have made, spacing the holes ½ inch apart.
5. Demonstrate the running stitch pattern to the child.
6. When he has finished using one length of string, knot it on the back side of the picture so it will not come undone. Start the next color.

## A Large Cardboard Box

One of the best toys you can provide for a three-year-old child is an empty cardboard box large enough for him to climb into—approximately 24 by 36 inches. The box quickly becomes a private corner for sitting, resting, or playing. It becomes a stimulant for fantasy play and can change rapidly from a house to a car to a rocket ship. The box usually falls apart before the child's interest wanes. One box, after assuming multiple roles, reverted back to its original purpose. My daughter climbed in, pulled the flaps over, and said, "I'm ready now, Mommy. Send me to Grandma."

# Four to Five Years Old

The four-year-old child is sophisticated and competent in comparison to his younger counterparts. Playing with friends is an important part of his day, so activities which can be shared are best. Board games, constructing products, and elaborate fantasy play are three popular choices.

## Board Games

Board games for the four- to five-year-old should require no reading skills. A first board game can be confined to matching colors. Games can get more complicated as your child's skills increase (e.g., counting, matching letters).

*Materials*
2 to 4 Fisher-Price little people (or any other figure that can be moved around the board— e.g., dinosaurs, soldiers, pennies)

8- by 11-inch file folder
markers of five different colors
index cards
rubber band

*Procedure*
1. Open the file folder. Draw a 2-inch square in the lower left-hand corner and write the word *START* (as in the illustration).
2. Draw a winding road from one end of the file folder to the other.
3. Mark off ½-inch squares and color each one, alternating the five different marker colors.
4. At the upper left-hand corner, draw a house, tree, cookies, or some other goal.
5. Cut the index cards into rectangles, 2 inches by 1 inch, making 40 squares.
6. Color each card, making eight cards of each color. Shuffle the cards.

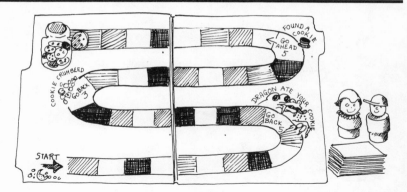

*Rules*

1. Players take turns drawing a card from the deck and moving their playing pieces to the nearest square of the matching color. The first to arrive at the goal wins.
2. As the child becomes adept at moving his piece around the board and going in the right direction, you can increase the complexity of the game. For example:
   a. You can designate certain squares as "traps." If you land on a particular square, you must go back three spaces. (The easiest way to designate a particular square as a trap is to put an X through it.)
   b. Anyone who lands on a square already occupied goes ahead to the next square of the same color.
   c. As your child becomes comfortable with counting, a die can be substituted for the color cards. Each person throws the die and moves the number of squares indicated.
   d. Letter squares can be substituted for color squares, and the matching deck can consist of letters of the alphabet. Do not use all letters of the alphabet at once.

## Wooden Products

One of the best gifts for a four-year-old is a bag of wood pieces in different sizes and shapes. Selections can be purchased which are already carefully sanded; unsanded scraps can usually be salvaged from a lumberyard for little or no cost. Either way, they provide the best play

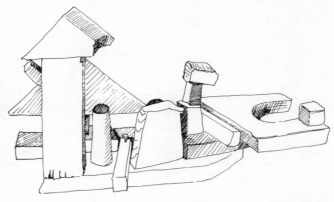

value for your money. Boats, castles, swords, and miniature furniture are just a small sample of the possible items that can be constructed from the wood. Just give the child the sanded wooden scraps and some glue, and he will make "sculptures" that will surpass your expectations. (Note: These creations are really nice gifts for grandparents or siblings, if the child is willing to part with them.)

## Clay

This recipe for homemade clay allows the child to make sculptures or holiday decorations that will last and can be displayed or given as gifts.

*Materials*
4 cups flour
1½ cups water
1 cup salt

bowl
rolling pin
cookie cutters

*Procedure*
1. Mix all ingredients together.
2. Knead the dough for ten minutes.
3. Roll out the dough to ¼ inch thick.
4. Form shapes or cut out shapes with cookie cutters.
5. Bake in 250° oven for two hours or until hard.
6. Let cool for at least one hour.

7. Paint forms with water or oil-base paint.
(Note: If making decorations to hang on Christmas trees, make a hole in the top of the shape before baking.)

## Dress Up

Trying on roles is like trying on hats: each one makes you feel different and results in different behavior. Children portray the adults with whom they are most familiar. Watching yourself reflected in the behavior of a child is revealing, funny, and sometimes surprising. This is an activity he will enjoy by himself or with a friend. Just provide the children with old adult clothing such as ties, hats, shoes, scarfs, dresses, shirts, and belts. Aluminum foil is one of the most versatile objects for constructing quick costumes which do not have to last long. An aluminum crown or a chest shield can easily turn a child into a king or knight.

## Puppets

Puppets are easy to construct and fun to use. Two simple puppets are the stick puppet and the finger puppet.

*Stick Puppet Materials*
sandwich-size brown
   paper bag
ice-cream stick
marker
yarn
glue

*Procedure*
1. Have the child decorate the bag, drawing a face and gluing on yarn for the hair.
2. Inflate the bag slightly.
3. Insert the stick a quarter of the way into the bag.

4. Tie a piece of yarn around the bottom of the bag and the stick.

*Finger Puppet Materials*
felt in a solid color
needle
thread
marker

*Procedure*
1. Fold the piece of felt in half.
2. Place the child's middle finger next to the fold.
3. Trace an enlarged outline of the finger.
4. Cut it out.
5. Thread a needle. Demonstrate a running stitch for the child.
6. Let the child sew the open seam,
7. Draw a face with a marker or sew on wool hair and button eyes.

# IX

# Television—The Mechanical Toy

From the first time a toddler turns the dial and sees a moving, talking image appear on the screen, it becomes easy for her to get "hooked" on television. I have observed homes in which the television was on all day, whereas in others viewing was restricted to specific programs. The overwhelming presence of television cannot be disputed. All of the homes I visited contained at least one television and many contained more than one. Nielsen verifies my small sample survey. According to a nationwide study, 98 percent of all homes in the United States contain one television, and 46 percent contain two or more.

Like toys, television can entertain and educate. However, good toys encourage a child to "learn while doing"; television viewing is a passive activity. Psychologists and educators are asking questions about the impact of television viewing on the pattern of experiences and development of young children. They do not know all the answers, but some of the available information is alarming.

**How much and when do young children watch television?** According to the 1977 Nielsen survey of 50,000 homes in the United States, the average child between two and five years of age watches 26½ hours of television each week. That is three hours and fifty minutes of viewing per day! In addition, the greatest percentage of two- to five-year old children are watching programs (see the table) during prime time (7:00–10:00 P.M.). The family is home together during the evening hours, but parents are usually exhausted from working all day, and watching television clearly demands less than playing, conversing or reading.

## Television Viewing Patterns of Children 2–5 Years of Age

| Day | Time | Percentage of Audience 2–5 Years Old |
|---|---|---|
| Mon.–Sat. Sunday | 8:00–11:00 P.M.* 7:00–11:00 P.M. | 22% |
| Mon.–Fri. | 4:30–7:30 P.M. | 20% |
| Sat. and Sun. | 7:00 A.M.–1:00 P.M. | 13% |
| Sat. Sun. | 1:00–8:00 P.M. 1:00–7:00 P.M. | 9% |
| Mon.–Sun. | 11:00 P.M.–1:00 A.M. | 1% |
| Remainder | | 15% |

*Prime time

According to Nielsen, the most popular prime time programs for children two to eleven years old* in 1977 were as follows:

"Happy Days"
"Laverne and Shirley"
"Six Million Dollar Man"
"Donny and Marie"
"Wonderful World of Disney"
"The Hardy Boys"
"Eight Is Enough"

"Three's Company"
"Wonder Woman"
"What's Happening!!"
"Welcome Back, Kotter"
"Starsky and Hutch"
"Tabitha"
"Bionic Woman"
"Logan's Run"

*Breakdowns for children two to five years old are not available.

This list, although diverse, offers little that a two- to five-year-old child would understand or benefit from viewing. As children get older, the amount of viewing increases, so that by the end of the twelfth grade the child will have spent more time in front of a television than in a classroom. These patterns also mean that in a given year a child is exposed to more than 20,000 commercials!

**What do children see on television?** Prime-time commercial television is geared to the teenage population. Most programs contain heavy doses of sexual innuendo and/or violence. Daytime "adult" shows consist primarily of soap operas, game shows, and talk shows. Although these offer little that would normally attract the attention of the preschooler, the content of the soap operas and the hysterical quality of the contestants on game shows make them questionable choices for even chance exposures.

Saturday mornings are considered the "children's hour." From 7:00 A.M. to noon, cartoons dominate the network program schedules. These interchangeable cartoons are action-packed sequences aimed at children in the two- to eleven-year age range. The plots are sparse and the characters go from one violent interaction to another. Dr. George Gerbner, a University of Pennsylvania psychologist, found that cartoons contain six times as many violent sequences as adult shows. Other researchers have found that there is a definite increase in the amount of aggressive behavior exhibited by children who have watched violent scenes on television.

Another major problem with network television is the number, content, and style of commercials. Federal regulations allow 9½ minutes of commercials for every hour of television during prime time and Saturday and Sunday morning programming. During weekly children's programs the number of commercials permitted rises to 12 minutes per hour, and at all other times 16 minutes per hour of commercials are allowed. Most advertisements during children's programs sell cereals, candy, and toys. The frequency of toy advertising increases dramatically before the holiday season. Even the more sedate shows such as "Romper Room" and "Captain Kangaroo" have the lead character introducing products to the audience. During cartoon shows, commercials may be animated, making them almost indistinguishable from the show for the young child. In fact, studies have found that children between five and eleven years of age have difficulty differentiating commercial messages from programs. For the child under the age of five, such distinctions may not exist.

## Public Television

The Children's Television Workshop, a nonprofit organization founded in 1968, has designed and produced two of the highest-quality products available to children: "Sesame Street" and "Electric Company." The goal of each program is to educate as well as entertain. Although both are theoretically designed for the "disadvantaged" child, they appeal to children of diverse backgrounds and ages.

"Sesame Street" is designed for the preschooler. Through the use of animation, puppets, and a regular group of people who "live" on Sesame Street, the program teaches numbers, letters, and beginning word recognition skills. In addition, situations are presented that show characters talking about feelings and solving problems through verbal rather than physical means.

The "Electric Company" reaches for the child in the early elementary school grades who is having difficulty mastering reading. This series is more action-packed than Sesame Street and even has superheroes of its own: Letterman and Spiderman.

Both series are fast-paced, professional products. They clearly illustrate that television can hold the interest of the young child without violence and can be educational as well as entertaining.

Reruns of "Mister Rogers' Neighborhood" can be found on most public television stations. This program has a much slower pace than the Children's Television Workshop products. The central figure, Mr. Rogers, is a soft-spoken, gentle man who talks to his audience as if there were guests in his home. Each show consists of a fantasy sequence acted out by puppets and an "educational" sequence during which children are shown how to make something or are given information about a topic that would interest them, such as space travel. Mr. Rogers routinely discusses feelings and problems common to all children. He clearly likes and respects children, and this warm feeling is transmitted to the viewers.

Television, like a book, exposes children to values, role models, and ethnic and sexual stereotypes. In contrast to storytime, children often watch television alone, and the content is not interpreted by an adult. They may see and hear things that confuse or frighten them or contradict what they experience in their own homes. In addition, they are bombarded by incorrect speech patterns ("he don't" and "ain't" are two of the more popular errors).

Any adult who has tried to get the attention of a child while she is watching a program can testify that children watch television with an intensity which is scary. Although it is difficult to assess the impact of each program on a child, viewing should be supervised by selecting programs carefully.

## Selecting Programs for Children

If you cannot state with certainty how much time the child in your care spends watching television each day, conduct your own survey. Every time the television is turned on record the time, the program, who selected the program, who watches the program, and when the television is turned off. You will quickly discover how much time is actually spent watching television in your home. The amount may be more than you anticipate. One discovery I made was that once the television is turned on, it tends to remain on for long periods regardless of the programs.

One of the accomplishments of the television industry is the wide variety of programs available to the viewer. Options, however, are only useful if you exercise them and carefully select what the child watches. Decide the maximum amount of viewing time you think the child should be allowed each day. If she is awake twelve hours each day, three hours of television viewing means she is spending 25 percent of her waking time watching television! I think that is too much. Once you determine what is a reasonable amount for your family, be firm and consistent. In some homes, preschoolers are only allowed to watch programs on the public television channel. (Watching "Sesame Street" and the "Electric Company" each day amounts to ninety minutes of television viewing.) In other homes preschoolers are allowed to watch early-morning commercial programs, as well as prime-time shows with the adults in the family. This quickly brings the total amount of time spent watching television up to the three-hour mark.

After deciding on the maximum amount of time you will allow, decide which programs are suitable for the child. Children should not make their own selections when they are two to five years of age. You may offer a choice between two shows you have already judged suitable, but you must do the initial selection and screening.

The best way to determine if a program is suitable for a child is to watch at least one segment of the series. You can judge if the characters treat each other in ways you consider acceptable and if the attitudes and situations portrayed are those you want the child exposed to. Once you have decided that a series is suitable for the child, do not leave her alone to cope with all she may see. Even if you cannot watch television with her, talk about what she sees. Children must be taught to question and evaluate what they see. Discuss whether people can really fly, jump over buildings, or smash doors with their hands. Suggest different strategies a character might have used to solve her problem. Discuss the purpose of commercials and the techniques used to make products appealing.

And finally, inform others who are responsible for the care of the child (e.g., baby-sitters, grandparents) about your rules for television viewing. It will not always work, but you should try to exert as much control over television viewing as you would over any other factor which could influence the child's development.

Concern about the quality and impact of television programs and commercials on audiences has stimulated the organization of several nonprofit consumer groups. Two of the more influential organizations, Action for Children's Television (ACT) and the National Association for Better Broadcasting (NABB), have testified before congressional committees investigating gratuitous violence and the type and number of commercials shown during children's programming. In addition, NABB annually publishes capsule reviews of network and public television offerings. Since prime-time program turnover is so rapid today, it is difficult to keep any listing current. However, shows that are no longer seen during the evening hours are often relegated to the late afternoon, when they are likely to draw a large preschool and school-age audience. The following NABB reviews are designed to serve as an initial screening guide for parents. However, what is appropriate for viewing by one family may not be appropriate for another family. These brief reviews should not replace your critical evaluations of the programs viewed by members of your family.

## NABB Guide to Television for the Family

### Commercial Network Children's Shows and Selected Syndicated Programs

**ABC Afterschool Specials**—monthly, afternoons. Probably the best entertainment for children available anywhere in TV. Producer Martin Tahse is an expert and conscientious craftsman. The stories are relevant and entertaining, constructed so as to appeal to the audience and make a point. For junior-high level; well worth family time.

**Adventures of Gilligan**—Syndicated. A silly, inept animated reconstruction of the original silly and inept live-action series. No value of any kind.

**Animals, Animals, Animals**—ABC. An excellent show. It may be too fast-paced for young children. It is like an animal magazine, including history, art, mythology. Sources, pictures, and narration are top quality. It is interesting to have animals put in a broader framework (time, history) rather than just show how they live today.

**Baggy Pants/Nitwits**—NBC. "Baggy Pants" is a routine animated presentation of Charles Chaplin. It is slapstick in treatment. "The Nitwits" fills the other half of the show, with Arte Johnson and Ruth Buzzi doing the voices of Tyrone and Gladys, roughly patterned from their characters in "Laugh-In." Many puns and wisecracks. Not much to recommend.

**Bang-Bang Lapalooza** (Archies and Sabrina)—NBC. Alternating segments of "The Archies" and "Sabrina," with the thin and tired action fortified by canned applause. The animated characters emphasize male/female stereotypes.

**Batman/Tarzan Hour**—CBS. Although some of the man-on-man violence has been removed, these Batman sequences still proclaim to present "the greatest array of villains the world has ever seen." The tongue-in-cheek treatment is lost on child audiences. The Tarzan cartoons that occupy the second half of the hour involve Tarzan and his animal friends in all sorts of grotesque and crime-ridden situations. The whole hour is an illustration of CBS irresponsibility to child viewers.

**Batman** (live action)—Syndicated. Violent, grotesque, preoccupied with crime. Sometimes morbid, with a distorted value system. Elementary school youngsters do not see this as satire. Totally unsuitable for children.

**Big Blue Marble**—Syndicated. Now aired by 160 public and commercial stations in the United States and by more than 60 overseas outlets, "Big Blue Marble" has 78 completed episodes, with 26 more in production. The series has won practically all of television's top awards. NABB, having previewed two episodes of the shows to debut in September, affirms its conclusion that this is the finest series for youngsters ever created. It is produced with the basic objective of fostering goodwill and understanding among youngsters of different countries and cultures. The program is produced by ITT as a public service. Robert Wiemer is the executive producer.

**Bugs Bunny/Road Runner**—CBS; syndicated under other titles. Traditional cartoons originally made by adults for other adults and intended for theatrical release. The fast pace and expert production tend to build an intense appeal. However, to a younger child the content is still chase-and-hit and bomb and fall-off-the-cliff. The program is a succession of bad examples presented in a favorable light.

**C.B. Bears**—NBC. This is a hodgepodge of questionable animated entertainment segments wedged between commercials for sugar cereals, lollipops, candy bars, and toys that are frightening to anyone with an active interest in child welfare. The whole thing is a Hanna-Barbera product of the type that has brought down the wrath of the just on Saturday morning television. Chases, explosions, falls, crashes—all without visible consequences, and most without discernible story continuity.

**Call It Macaroni**—Syndicated. This is an imaginative series expertly produced by Westinghouse Broadcasting.

It uses a lot of what television does best. Youngsters are taken from their own environment to participate with adults in activities in exciting and totally different surroundings. Emphasis is on caring and supportive relationships, and on adventure. "Call It Macaroni" involves children in real experiences that are ordinarily limited to dreams or fantasies.

**Captain Kangaroo**—CBS, daily. It takes four or five years for small fry to grow into and grow out of "Captain Kangaroo," and Bob Keeshan as the Captain has done a super job of befriending many millions of the nation's children through the cycles of their formative years. Warm and timely, changing with the times, the program retains constant values in content and production.

**Children's Film Festival**—CBS. Marvelous films dealing with children of other countries. A consistently engrossing and worthwhile series. Highly recommended.

**Dusty's Treehouse**—Syndicated. A beguiling show involving puppets and real-life situations. Concerned without being preachy. Characters are humorous and spunky. They make mistakes and learn from these experiences.

**Emergency Plus Four**—Syndicated. This cartoon show exploits the interests of youngsters in live-action programs with similar backgrounds. The young characters in this series are often in peril. The real-life informational quality is lost entirely.

**Fat Albert and the Cosby Kids**—CBS. Within the clutter of the Saturday kid-vid ghetto, this program is a shining example of what goodwill and talent can accomplish. A superior program that depicts black youngsters as appealing and realistic people. The characterization and story qualities are excellent. Bill Cosby in relation to children is a delight.

**The Flintstones**—Syndicated. Hanna-Barbera produced 167 episodes of this series, and they have been rerun interminably in many communities. The cartoons are ingenious and funny, but sex stereotypes are prevalent and often are offensive. The offensiveness is heightened by repeated presentation.

**The Froozles**—Syndicated. This five-times-per-week show for children is an ambitious enterprise of RKO General. It is a combination of puppets and live action. The daily schedule includes "window to faraway places," segments that cover appealing visits to foreign locations. The program is imaginative, with a bright and cheerful tone backed by professional production. Long-time children's show producer Sally Baker is writer-producer.

**Grape Ape**—ABC. Grotesque, ugly, and mindless cartoons.

**Hong Kong Phooey**—NBC. Fourth-rated animated Charlie Chan–type series with silly, impossible stories. Background is crime and violence. Hero bungles his way to success over villains. Low-quality artwork and production.

**Hot Fudge**—Syndicated. This program combines puppets and live performers in a series that is both entertaining and responsible. It is a warm and lively show that deals with children's emotional development and well-being. "Hot Fudge" is promoted as a program that satisfies the child's need for entertainment, as well as the broadcaster's obligation to provide constructive experiences. It meets both objectives.

**In the News**—CBS. Brief segments produced by CBS News, aired between regular morning programs. Timely and interesting, but generally surrounded by programming that is mediocre or worse.

**Jabberjaw**—ABC. Sharks, rock music, and other gimmicks combined with crime-oriented plots and offensive teenage stereotypes.

**Jeannie Cartoons**—Syndicated. A shallow and almost mindless animated version of the original "I Dream of Jeannie" live-action series. At best a waste of time.

**The Jetsons**—Syndicated. The space gadgetry in these cartoons is fun, but the people are stereotypes and unpleasant models of human behavior.

**Krofft Super Show**—ABC. A conglomeration of segments strung together in a gimmicky format designed to hold the hour together as a single program unit. Standard stereotypes. Slapstick humor with problems solved by physical superpower. As a whole the show is noisy and tasteless. It exploits the response of children to flash and motion and glitter.

**Land of the Lost**—NBC. This features fascinating prehistoric dinosaurs, but the show deals in trite plots, gimmicks, and unpleasant family characterizations. Consistent peril to youngsters rules it out for very young viewers. A waste of time for others.

**Lassie**—Syndicated. It is difficult to evaluate this as a whole, because the durable dog has run through several families, and there are a number of series making the rerun rounds. Some of the families provide more acceptable models than others. An important thing about the program as a whole, however, is that it was one of the first to hype its plots to attract larger and more diverse audiences. Although many adults remember Lassie as the prototype of lovable friends for children, many of the subsequent episodes contain frightening and heart-wrenching incidents in which the dog and children are in peril.

**Little Rascals**—Syndicated. Very dated, but these short films are still running in many communities. There is little appeal other than nostalgia. The racial stereotypes are offensive.

**Lost in Space**—Syndicated. Low-grade science fiction

in hour-long live action. Bad family pattern in that adults do not take care of the children, who are in turn constantly disobedient and undisciplined.

**Mario and the Magic Movie Machine**—CBS. This is no great shakes as entertainment, but it does have its resourceful moments. Under Mario's direction the movie machine comes forth with film clips of personalities and events of varying interest. Certainly the show is a step up from the common level of Saturday A.M. mediocrity. It is originated by Westinghouse and Post Newsweek stations.

**Mickey Mouse Club**—Syndicated. This ambitious series of daily half-hour programs is an important and highly entertaining update of the original Disney "Mickey Mouse Club" that set standards for children's programming beginning in 1955. The new production and new approach have corrected the one glaring flaw of the original show, which had little if any racial or ethnic integration. Because of the financial costs, new production has slowed, but even with its dependence on reruns this is one of the few quality shows for children.

**Muggsy**—NBC. "Muggsy" is a dramatic series about a thirteen-year-old girl who lives under the care of her brother in a rundown section of a modern city. It is an outstanding program made with care and a good feeling for the participants. Muggsy meets a variety of people, each of whom is real and human, as are their problems. Good ethnic city mix and good understanding of child-level interests, with appropriate themes and plots. Action and situations are seen through the eyes of a youngster, but without its being a youngster's world alone.

**Oddball Couple**—Syndicated. The difference between this and the "Odd Couple" live-action series is that these cartoons are trivial and grotesque, and the characters constantly trick and outwit each other. Thus the show is unpleasant and mediocre.

**The Pink Panther**—NBC. Made by adults essentially

for adults, this is stylish and funny, but often unsuitable for children. Violence and crime themes; bombs and explosives.

**Popeye**—Syndicated under various show titles. "Popeye" and "The Three Stooges" were the earliest fun shows for children that led teachers and parents to see a connection between children's interaction and television models. These cartoons date way back, but even the oldest are currently being shown. They are extremely violent. People hurting each other is the theme of every cartoon. Although nostalgic for parents, this is precisely an unfortunate teaching picture for young children.

**Porky Pig**—Syndicated under various program names. Again, we have here characters and cartoons familiar to parents and grandparents who saw them when they were originated for theater release. In large doses, these are not suitable for children. They contain much violence. Characters are really offensive stereotypes who ridicule people.

**Romper Room**—Syndicated format. Thanks to ACT's efforts, "Romper Room" no longer devotes its content to plugging toys and other consumer products. The teacher is a different person in each market, so the program will vary in quality from city to city. The format of games and information is harmless, but it is not structured to be helpful to children.

**Schoolhouse Rock**—ABC (between shows). These short segments include "Grammar Rock" and other bits designed to teach math and history. Some work better than others. The historical ones are superficial and convey little information. Most are delightful—fast-paced, funny, and catchy—especially "Grammar Rock." However, the NABB committee cannot recommend *anything* among the surrounding ABC weekend morning schedule, which children will have to watch if they are to see these brief transitional segments.

**Shazam/ISIS Hour**—CBS. In the first half-hour the show's teenage hero turns into Captain Marvel. In the second part Isis is a high school science teacher who calls upon supernatural powers from ancient Egypt to transform herself into a flying superwoman. Both of these shows are based on comic-book plots, with superpowers delivering youngsters from extreme and bizarre perils. Unlike Filmation's "Fat Albert," which delivers prosocial concepts as content integral to the story with wit and charm, "Shazam" and "Isis" too often deliver copy-book morals whose connection with the plot is stilted and artificial.

**Space Academy**—CBS. This is a Prescott-Scheimer live-action production based on outer-space gadgetry. The cast is racially integrated, and the performances and scripts are on an unusually adequate level for Saturday morning shows.

**Special Treat**—NBC; monthly in afternoons. These are varied programs of unusual quality. In addition to drama, other arts are featured in some of the productions. The show has a special appeal for junior high students, as well as for adults. Some of the episodes are new; some are repeated; all are worthwhile.

**Speed Buggy**—NBC. This was the original idea that walked over to ABC and became "Wonderbug." That show became popular, so now this old cartoon series has been disinterred for reruns on NBC. It is composed of silly crime stories.

**Speed Racer**—Syndicated. This animated monstrosity is an example of the worst that television has ever produced. It is the ultimate in crime, evil characters, cruelty, and destruction. Even so, some independent and network-affiliated broadcasters flaunt their irresponsibility by stripping this in five days per week in afternoon hours when children are the least supervised and the most available. NABB strongly recommends that parents keep this out of the reach of their children.

**Superman/Batman/Aquaman**—Syndicated. Three of the worst cartoon series ever produced, combined in a single program package to heighten their violence-for-kicks effectiveness.

**Sylvester and Tweety**—CBS. The cat is always trying to hurt the bird, but he gets hurt himself. There is a lot of physical action related to burning, hitting, blowing up, boiling, etc. Unattractive and mediocre.

**The Three Stooges**—Syndicated. Research on the behavior of children and innumerable complaints from parents and teachers have documented "The Three Stooges" as a prime incitement to unruly behavior by children everywhere. Indiscriminate unmotivated violence, perceived as such by young audiences to whom slapstick is just a word. This show is the very worst of its kind. (See also "Popeye.")

**Thunder**—NBC. This live-action program has its positive points, but the "prosocial messages" are often dragged in by contrived devices. There are scenic pluses, and the kids are attractive, but the writers lack the talent to put together a valid creative production. The horse Thunder is beautiful, but what can a horse do but run and rear? His feats in this show are too far out and incredible even for the small fry to assimilate.

**Tom and Jerry**—Syndicated. Although the newer episodes of these cartoons have been softened by making the two characters into friends instead of unremitting enemies, the show is still noisy and full of slapstick violence. Not adequate as entertainment for children.

**Underdog**—Syndicated. One of the worst of the old crime-ridden series that have been rejected by responsible broadcasters. Parents beware. Some stations are still airing this rubbish.

**Valley of the Dinosaurs**—Syndicated. Crude and illogical dialogue and story treatment. Natural catastrophes and other perils dominate the action.

**Vegetable Soup**—Syndicated. This show has a magazine format, and it is the most successful among a number of programs designed to encourage youngsters of different backgrounds to be comfortable together. Features include stories, cartoons, recipes, and a variety of people in real situations. Worth looking for.

**Wacko**—CBS. Live action; weird costumes; weird sets. The show is noise, bolstered by rock music. At least they got the name right.

**Weekend Special**—ABC. This show is an oasis of quality in the Saturday morning desert. It includes well-produced short stories, multipart novels, and other materials such as the recent musical cartoon about the human body. This episode impressed on youngsters the dangers of smoking and of nonnutritional diets.

**Woody Woodpecker**—ABC. Woody, in his latest incarnation, is the gentlest of the regular cartoon characters. The emphasis is on cuteness and ingenuity rather than violence. Woody is an appealing tease, not a menace.

**Young Sentinels**—NBC. Another Prescott-Scheimer show, this time animated, and this time built around the superpowers of the chief characters. Such problems as the North Pole vanishing and the imminent destruction of the world are resolved by power, not reason or right.

## Public Television Children's Shows

The majority of the superior programs for children are still broadcast on public television. The most famous are still those programs made to teach academic skills to "deprived" youngsters, such as "Sesame Street" and "Electric Company." They are a delight to almost all children and extremely competent teaching tools for all ages.

**Mister Rogers' Neighborhood** is an especially gentle and responsible show for preschoolers. It offers a calculated change from TV's usually frenetic pace.

**Once Upon a Classic** is a fine series of serialized dramatizations of classics and classic types of modern-day stories. Well-worn favorites are retold with such rich production and fidelity to the source that they become a pleasure for all the family to share.

There are a number of delightful programs that teach language and customs as bilingual/bicultural education. The most widely available are "Villa Allegre" and "Carrascolendas." These and other programs on public television provide guides for teachers and helpful materials for use at home and at school. Besides being constructive, these programs are fun to watch.

**Vision On,** produced by BBC, is designed to entertain hard-of-hearing youngsters. It covers a wide range of subject matter with a variety of techniques. It is a good example of television being used to its best advantage.

**Zoom,** popular over several seasons, is a kid-oriented variety show with lots of participation.

## Commercial Network Prime-Time Shows and Selected Syndicated Programs

**Adam 12**—Syndicated. Although this series depicts the police as competent professionals, it is now aired up to 10 times per week on some stations. Some episodes have a lot of criminal violence. As a regular diet for children, it adds up to a heavy dose of crime and police action.

**Alice**—CBS. This is one of the handful of series that have improved rather than followed the pronounced downward trend common to most of the networks' weekly situation comedies. It can be very funny, and the characters have grown beyond the stereotypes of last season's early episodes. Warm and appealing, with a rare touch of class.

**All in the Family**—CBS. Archie and company have sailed into heavy seas in some of their recent programs, e.g., the two-part rape attack on Edith, and Edith's rejection of God on the Christmas show. It is commendable and valuable to base comedy on serious themes, but the treatment must be more than superficial. Occasional "All in the Family" sequences come dangerously close to melodrama. But the show is provocative and fun to watch.

**America**—Syndicated. Alistair Cooke's distinguished series of documentaries is superior as a geographic and historical review, and as sheer entertainment as well. Well worth a second or third viewing.

**Animal World**—Syndicated. Much of this is a beautifully scenic presentation of wildlife in various locales, but at times the action and continuity appear to be contrived to heighten the dramatic impact. At any rate, it is a welcome relief from the game shows that clutter early evening hours.

**Baretta**—ABC. Robert Blake dominates a supercharged series that is tough, vengeful, and murderous. Baretta is an emotionally driven cop who operates as a loner, rather than as a member of a law enforcement team. There is an emphasis on rape and other forms of violent crime against helpless victims. NABB's suggestion: Parents should keep this out of the reach of youngsters. It is a deplorable prospect for future syndication for multiple-week showings in daytime hours.

**Barnaby Jones**—CBS. A routine gimmicky melodrama with Buddy Ebsen as a private eye. Not for kids.

**Barney Miller**—ABC. The situations presented in "Barney Miller" and some of the guest characters who drift in and out of the precinct headquarters may disturb some viewers, but this is a show where pathos and humor are mixed with great skill, and where cops are realistic without being cynical, compassionate without being maudlin, and outrageously funny without gimmicky props. Performances are superb.

**Big Valley**—Syndicated. Hour-long westerns now usually scheduled in late afternoons five times per week to catch the after-school youngsters. Excessive violence in many episodes. Story themes are often adult in treatment, unsuitable for children.

**Bonanza**—Syndicated. As westerns go, this is one of the best. Parents should know, however, that many episodes have excessive violence. Five hours a week are a heavy dose of such materials for youngsters.

**Candid Camera**—Syndicated. This is a contrived show that is often tasteless in its treatment of embarrassing situations.

**Cannon**—Syndicated. Sometimes interesting but essentially routine melodrama. Graphic violence makes this a frightening prospect for five-day-per-week airing in late afternoon or early evening hours when youngsters are the primary audience.

**Charlie's Angels**—ABC. We don't need to point out to anyone who has watched this program that it exploits women and uses every device to expose their physical appeals. It's a junior-grade Playboy or Penthouse. It has much violence and continuous sexual innuendo, except that the "innuendo" comes across like a neon billboard.

**Chips**—NBC. There could be no more dismal commentary on NBC programming than the fact that "Chips" is the sole survivor among eight new series launched by the network in September. This is fun and games on motorbikes at 80 miles per hour over the Los Angeles freeways and streets. A temptation for emulation by youngsters, without cautions of the realistic results of dangerous highway action. The stories are elemental and the dialogue sophomoric.

**Cousteau Specials**—PBS and Syndicated. Superb programs of rare beauty. Intermittently scheduled, but don't miss them.

**Directions**—ABC. A long-established quality feature aired for years over CBS. Provocative discussions of a wide variety of social problems.

**Donny and Marie**—ABC. Variety and music primarily for younger teens, but with an appeal for the entire family. The sets, costumes, and production are handsome and meticulous. The program, both in appearance and in content, has a cheerful, dressed-up tone that is a welcome variation from most of today's TV variety shows.

**Eight Is Enough**—ABC. An uneven show, but the story themes dip into current life-style situations, and come out on the side of family unity and affection. There is much emphasis on sexual topics, but the subplots cover a wide range. The writing seems to be more routine and less creative than in episodes of the preceding season. Cast and production are okay. NABB suggests that parents take a look to see if they are comfortable with this as family fare.

**Emergency One**—Syndicated. These programs are well produced and they have positive values in building awareness of paramedical and other helping services. For youngsters, on a daily basis, the series might be too heavy a dose of graphic and often frightening incidents.

**The F.B.I.**—Syndicated. Scheduled on some stations Monday through Friday, this series is totally unsuitable as regular fare for youngsters. "The F.B.I." is not only an illustration of the misuse of official support (by the F.B.I. itself), it is also excessively violent and sordid in story content. It is a dismal portrayal of the F.B.I. as our leading law enforcement body. More often than not solutions are achieved by sheer luck and last-second rescues of terrorized victims of criminals.

**Family**—ABC. This is an excellent dramatic series with a week-to-week involvement of members of the same family. The characters are consistent and the situations are credible. Sex is far from taboo, but it is not the dirty-words-on-the-alley-fence treatment of sex that is typical of the same network's "Three's Company," "Soap," or numerous other current series. "Family" is a good program for teens or older family members. Superior cast; superior production; superior scripts.

**Family Feud**—Syndicated. This is an "access time" game show that has a measure of warmth and fun, along with some challenges that bring viewers into an active involvement. O.K. for family viewing.

**Fantasy Island**—ABC. This show is built around a so-called fantasy situation in which participants live out their dreams and desires on an island operated by Ricardo Montalban. Unfortunately, the whole thing is contrived and unimaginative. The stories are shoddy and woefully lacking in creative quality.

**The Gong Show**—Syndicated. Crude and obnoxious. This will have to rise several fathoms to reach the bottom.

**Good Times**—CBS. This is a series about a family that happens to be black. In its first seasons it featured the family unit in realistic but warm and human situations. It was an appealing show and it was successful both in creative qualities and in the ratings. Then the producers dropped the talented John Amos as the father, and then they messed around with the format and the characterizations to such an extent that Esther Rolle dropped out in protest over the insensitive treatment of the original premise. Now we have a family with no stabilizing head except the near-stereotype J.J., who is more a comedian than a responsible leader in the home.

**Lou Grant**—CBS. Sometimes ponderous, but essentially a quality dramatic show built around Lou Grant's impressive talents. Top cast. Expert production covering its newspaper background.

**Gunsmoke**—Syndicated. Matt, Doc, Festus, and Kitty (and Kitty's "girls") are now available to children on a five-times-per-week schedule on many stations. There are innumerable episodes. The NABB committee calls the attention of parents to the fact that many of these episodes, particularly those from the earlier years, have extreme violence and sordid story situations. Then there is the background of the Long Branch saloon where the prostitutes under Kitty's wing live in comfort and friendship while their more chaste sisters battle the elements and loneliness in scattered cabins "way out on the prairie."

**Hall of Fame**—NBC, intermittent schedule. This has been another typically outstanding season for Hallmark's "Hall of Fame." There have been four new productions, beginning with Carroll O'Connor's "The Last Hurrah" in November. The concluding show is a repeat of the delightful "Peter Pan" (March 16) which was created for the series' Silver Jubilee in 1976. This is the show's 27th season.

**Happy Days**—ABC. Synthetic nostalgia with an unreal and trivial background of high schoolers in the 1950s. Funny and witty. Good fun.

**The Hardy Boys**—NBC. The Hardy Boys are juvenile adventure seekers. The programs are not gruesome, and there is only a small quotient of graphic violence, but the plots are concerned with thefts, attempted assassinations, and continual danger to the youngsters from criminal activities. The NABB committee suggests to parents that they evaluate this for possible unsuitability for their children's viewing.

**Harry O**—Syndicated. David Janssen as a private eye in violence-ridden episodes designed to terrify and shock. The situations deal with dope, corruption, sadism, casual sex, and various forms of brutality and murder. The view of life is distorted and sick. Not recommended for children under any circumstances.

**Hawaii Five-O**—CBS. This program has already been sold for future interminable reruns on many stations. It will almost certainly be aired five times per week in late-afternoon and early-evening hours. There has been some token reduction in graphic terror and violence in current network episodes, but the package that will be released for children's daily entertainment is saturated with gory and sordid incidents. "Hawaii Five-O" is traditionally the most violent television series produced since the infamous "The Untouchables."

**Hee Haw**—Syndicated. Unabashed corny country humor and music. Resourceful production.

**Hogan's Heroes**—Syndicated. This is still airing in late-afternoon and early-evening time periods five days per week. It adds up to a massive dose of war that is fun for kids who have no recollection of the horrors of the Nazi prison camps on which this series is based.

**Hollywood Squares**—Syndicated. Possibly the best known of all game shows, this has slick production and a lot of glitter. It also has an overdose of commercial exploitation and double-entendre titillation. A matter of taste, but the NABB committee think that children should not be exposed.

**In Search of...**—Syndicated. A well-produced and often challenging semidocumentary that explores mysteries that have baffled mankind. An Alan Landsburg production of more than ordinary interest and appeal.

**Insight**—Syndicated. Approaching its 18th year of production, "Insight," as far as we know, is television's longest-running dramatic series. Father Ellwood Keiser, head of Paulist Productions, and producer of "Insight," refers to the theme of the program as "God-centered humanism permeated with love, compassion, and hope." Scripts, performances, and production qualities are first-rate.

**Ironside**—Syndicated. Interesting melodrama for adults, but too violent and crime-oriented for youngsters in its customary late-afternoon, five-times-per-week schedule.

**The Jeffersons**—CBS. This series, originally a spinoff from "All in the Family," has mellowed in its earlier presentation of Jefferson as a brash bigot. It is funny, and it is often appealing. Essentially, however, it deals with caricature rather than warm characterization.

**Kojak**—Syndicated. Tough, hard-hitting melodrama. Subject matter and violence make it unsuitable for youngsters.

**Last of the Wild**—Syndicated. Lorne Greene does a top job as narrator for this entertaining wildlife series. The photography is beautiful.

**Laverne and Shirley**—ABC. Funny lightweight comedy, but sexual innuendos make it questionable for youngsters. A matter of taste.

**Let's Make a Deal**—Syndicated. A five-times-per-week play on greed and frenzy.

**Little House on the Prairie**—NBC. As its audience rating has grown, this program has gained in characterizations and production qualities. The stories are strong, with exceptional sensitivity in dealing with value systems and interpersonal relationships. An excellent series for regular family viewing.

**Love, American Style**—Syndicated. The point of the show is to trivialize relationships between men and women. Taste is often stretched to the breaking point. Not for youngsters.

**The Love Boat**—ABC. This is a new hour-long show

for retarded adults who still think that the height of comedy is a series of events that frustrate the consummation of a newlywed couple's marriage. Several concurrent story lines run through each episode, but we'd challenge anyone to remember any an hour after the show had ended.

**Mannix**—Syndicated. Rough and tough crime drama, with sex thrown in for the pseudo sophisticates. Psycho criminals involved in sordid situations.

**Marcus Welby, M.D.**—Syndicated. Superior casting and first-rate production. Entertaining for adults, but a caution is due regarding this and other "doctor" shows. It is the nature of these programs to depict rare and serious ailments, thus building for regular viewers a distorted impression of the dangers and woes of ordinary living.

**M\*A\*S\*H**—CBS. One of TV's handful of outstanding weekly series. Sharp wit, combined with a moving and compassionate treatment of the stupidities and brutalities of war. The cast is superb. Sex is handled with humor and from balanced points of view, a marked contrast with TV's current obsession with sex as a crude and public exhibition.

**Medical Center**—Syndicated. This series often shows distorted melodramatic treatment of medical situations. It could feed on fears, thus generating undue alarm and feelings of insecurity.

**Mod Squad**—Syndicated. Distributed widely as a five-times-per-week program in early-evening hours, "Mod Squad" indoctrinates hundreds of thousands of children with misconceptions about the proper roles of adolescents in regard to crime and to law enforcement. Episodes are often engrossed in graphic violence and sordid story material. The loyalties and affections between the three youthful characters are appealing.

**Mary Tyler Moore Show**—Syndicated. Watching

reruns of "MTM" is not only fun and nostalgic; it illustrates the vast superiority of some past series over much of the current season's froth and drivel.

**The Muppet Show**—Syndicated. NABB cited this program as "the most creative, entertaining, and refreshing new program of the 1976-77 season." It is still superb in many aspects. Production-wise it is incredibly skillful. But sound-wise it appears to have added some decibels to a degree of occasional stridency.

**Bob Newhart Show**—CBS. As with the "Mary Tyler Moore Show," this is a family program about adults. It is funny and warm. Expert production. Quality scripts.

**Night Gallery**—Syndicated. Now often scheduled several days per week in pre-bedtime hours for children, this is a terrifying nightmare-producer of the first magnitude.

**One Day at a Time**—CBS. An intriguing show that is sometimes questionable in its approach to social values. Although Ann and her daughters are appealing, the peripheral characters are often clowns or stereotypes who lend superficial or unreal elements to the solutions to very real social problems. Role models are disturbing.

**Operation Petticoat**—ABC. Superficial comedy based on gag-type situations stemming from nurses aboard a decrepit World War II submarine.

**Police Story**—NBC; intermittent schedule. Immeasurably superior to "Police Woman" on the same network, "Police Story" has been bounced around by the network brass who believe (possibly correctly) that they can sell more audience digits to advertisers by the visual exposure of Angie Dickinson's anatomy and the details of sordid behavior than by the presentation of a valid and realistic drama or melodrama legitimately based on violent criminal activity. More than ever, all three networks are illustrating their single-standard obsession with audience ratings regardless of social responsibility.

**Police Woman**—NBC. Star Angie Dickinson has announced publicly that she is leaving this show if the producers continue to force her into a role that is sexually demeaning and otherwise objectionable. Why did she wait so long? From its inception this has been a nasty program that is tasteless and offensive to the majority of viewers who believe that America's living rooms should not be the arenas for the display of gratuitous violence and semi-porno entertainment.

**Quincy**—NBC. Jack Klugman as a virtually infallible coroner who outshines the police in detecting and in solving violent homicides. On-camera violence is minimized, but story situations are morbid.

**The Rockford Files**—NBC. An episode will begin with humor and a tongue-in-cheek treatment of the characters and situations, then *whammo!*, the tone changes and everything is brutal and deadly serious. The way to survive, Rockford implies, is to trust almost anyone except the police. This is adult escapism—not for youngsters.

**The Rookies**—Syndicated. This long-running cop series is now offered in syndication and has been promoted as an "ideal" show for family viewing. The stories are unremittingly sordid and violent. They do not belong on the air at any time when children are a major proportion of viewers. Because of its promotion there is a special threat that irresponsible broadcasters will schedule this five times per week in afternoon or early-evening hours.

**Room 222**—Syndicated. A first-rate series with a thoughtful and entertaining approach to student-teacher issues. A natural and appealing treatment of racial integration.

**Sha Na Na**—Syndicated. A bright surprise of the new season that shows us that "access time" (early evening, non-network) need not be taken over by the customary blatant, noisy, often vulgar game and quiz shows that saturate these early hours. This variety show has more class and real entertainment in its half hour than most of network TV's hour-long weekly variety shows or specials.

**Six Million Dollar Man**—Syndicated. This show attracts millions of teens and children. It also illustrates a world full of evil and constant menace. In part, it is recycled Superman. Fantasy and reality are mixed, so that youngsters cannot distinguish between the two. Not recommended for children.

**Sixty Minutes**—CBS. This is sharp-edged, timely, and courageously bold. Plus all that, it is a surprise hit in the ratings—evidence again that maturity and substance are not necessarily anathema to commercial success. An immensely valuable and provocative program that illustrates what television can be when someone really tries.

**Star Trek**—Syndicated. Expert and imaginative production. The best of the space shows, thoughtfully written and excellently cast. Some episodes are too frightening for unattended children.

**Starsky and Hutch**—ABC. Although some of the overt violence has been statistically eliminated, this show is basically built for the presentation of crime and horror. It has dealt with such sick audience lures as prototypes of Manson and his "family" of male and female psychos. Starsky and Hutch are dangerous role models for impressionable youngsters.

**Streets of San Francisco**—Syndicated. A tough and brutal series of hour-long melodramas, with graphic portrayals of murder and other crimes. Highly unsuitable for youngsters.

**Three's Company**—ABC. This is for the woefully

inexperienced and the incurably immature who get their kicks from the two-gag situations of a boy (supposedly gay) sharing an apartment with two girls and the apartment manager whose wife is unable to persuade him to perform in bed.

**The Untouchables**—Syndicated. This brutal and irresponsible series is still in widespread circulation, so we need to include here a caution to parents about its availability to children. Critic John Crosby described this as "the worst program ever made for television." His evaluation still stands, although today's critics never look at it and never write about its menace.

**The Waltons**—CBS. "The Waltons," an enormous and durable success, still shows the involvement of its original creator, Earl Hamner. The characters have grown and changed as the family has moved into new times and situations. The basic appeal of the program remains centered on its dramatization of the strength of a family without dependence on economic affluence, and with room for individual differences.

**Welcome Back, Kotter**—ABC. Kotter is an unorthodox teacher, and many of the situations that evolve in his classroom are really funny. However, in essence this is a gimmick show that is escapism for school youngsters. Broad comedy with little depth. The sweathogs have no resemblance to any actual class, integrated or not.

**Lawrence Welk Show**—Syndicated. This sentimental airing of "old-fashioned" music holds it popularity year after year.

**What's Happening!!**—ABC. This continues to be an appealing program about a black family that is united and affectionate in a realistic modern urban world. Story situations and dialogue are thoughtful and provocative. The cast is excellent.

**Wild Kingdom**—NBC. This series is now in its

fifteenth season. The program itself illustrates real concern for wildlife, and it is consistently interesting and entertaining.

**The Wild, The Weird, and The Wonderful**—Syndicated. A new series of 26 half-hour color travel films produced by Hall and Halla Linker, who also produced the well known "Wonders of the World" programs that featured the adventures of "America's most traveled family" in familiar and remote areas throughout the world. The Linker quality in production and program content is well established. This will no doubt be an intriguing series worth seeking out among the jumble of exploitive game shows and other trivia that clutter the early-evening hours in most areas.

**Wild Wild West**—Syndicated. Parents beware. Episodes are often sordid, with brutality-for-thrills sequences that are a menace to children and unsuitable for anyone else. This is a kinky show that has become one of the most unsavory features of late-afternoon programming for the nation's youngsters.

**Wild World of Animals**—Syndicated. A superior series beautifully photographed, with apparently authentic portrayal of wildlife. Narration stresses information without contrived sensationalism.

**Wildlife in Crisis**—Syndicated. Thirty-nine fascinating half-hour episodes in color. This may be the most authentic and informative wildlife series ever filmed for television. Producer/narrator Norma Foster has put together a program that illustrates and analyzes the crises faced by endangered species. The endorsements by worldwide societies are imposing.

**Wonder Woman**—CBS. ABC dropped this, and CBS inexplicably picked it up. It's a comic-book show with far too much crime and violence for the child audiences it attracts. The acting is incredibly wooden. The whole thing is sexist and silly.

**Wonderful World of Disney**—NBC. These programs are consistently far above average in quality, but they are not always the last word in good family entertainment. The stories are worked into a salable framework. Sometimes the authenticity of classics is sacrificed to fit into the Disney image and appeal. Production values are exceptional.

**The World at War**—Syndicated. An excellent documentary of World War II in hour-long episodes. This is full of historic footage acquired from opposing forces in history's greatest war. For the perceptive, war is set forth with all its horrors. This series is not intended as *entertainment*. It is for mature audiences seeking a realistic view and understanding of immeasurable tragedy.

**World of Survival**—Syndicated. A wildlife series that features portrayal of species threatened with extinction through man's neglect. Produced with aid from the World Wildlife Fund.

# X

# Display and Storage of Toys

Toys can be a nuisance. They are left everywhere and we trip over them, step on them, and try to walk around them. Parents use many strategies to organize their children's toys. In some homes toys are kept in the bedroom and children are expected to play there. In other homes the den or family room may be turned over to the children and designated as a "playroom." Usually this means that the parents have given up trying to maintain order and have found a room they can close off when company visits. Manufacturers offer "toy chests" as aids in the display and storage of toys. There are also toy bags, hampers, and crates. All provide convenient locations to "dump" toys, but none are particularly appropriate from the child's point of view.

Children like to play near their parents. Even four-year-olds are rarely content to play in a room on a different floor or far removed from the adult areas of the home. During the course of the day, children make many overtures to their parents. They need help, reassurance, comfort, or information. These recurrent interactions require easy access to parents, who act as a resource for the child.

During my years of research with the Harvard Preschool Project, I learned that these frequent interactions between child and parent are important educational opportunities. They provide optimal "teachable moments" when parents can educate their child about the properties of a toy or use that toy to teach related concepts. These interactions allow adults to share knowledge with and expand the child's horizons by taking advantage of what the child is interested in at that moment. This informal method of instruction is very effective with children from birth to age five. How does this relate to the display and storage of toys? If children are expected to play in a bedroom or in a playroom, away from the adult centers of the home, the physical separation precludes the easy occurrence of "teachable moments." The most beautifully designed playroom is nothing more than a glorified playpen if a child is restricted to that one room. Children need access to their parents, and if parental expectations are realistic, children will be playing in many rooms of the house.

## Toy Centers in the Home

Do children need access to every room in the house? Should you turn over your home to your child? Let me answer emphatically *no*! However, if you want to maximize the child's use of his toys, make provisions for their display and storage in various rooms of your home. I am suggesting the designation of *toy centers* in the home's most commonly used rooms—for example, the kitchen, the television room or den, the child's bedroom, or any other room where adults spend a great deal of time. This does not mean that you should not declare a particular room off limits. Adults have rights too, and studies or other "adult only" rooms do not have to be made available for play.

## What Is a Toy Center?

A toy center is a fancy name for a closet, cabinet, shelf, or drawer you have allocated for the display and/or storage of toys. These locations in various rooms in the home are carefully selected to ensure that the child can see and reach his toys. They are also well organized so that he can put away his toys when he is finished playing. Toy centers increase the child's access to his toys and encourage him to use them.

## Clean-up Time

Parents frequently ask: "How can I get my child to put away his toys after using them?" The answer is easier to say than to do. Your demands must be reasonable and consistent and the task must not be too difficult.

The twelve-month-old child is typically the most cooperative (in this age range) at clean-up time. He is enthusiastic about this activity because it allows him to interact with you in what he thinks is a game or more play. However, he will remove toys as quickly as he replaces them as part of the same game.

As your child gets older, you expect him to clean up by himself. Although children never have any problem creating a mess, creating order out of it is often an overwhelming task for them. Frequently, they forget the task at hand and begin playing again. Putting toys away becomes even more difficult if the child has to transport them to a different room. This task will be accomplished most efficiently if you help and direct your child and provide "toy centers" in various rooms in your home.

## The Bedroom

When a child is a newborn, display and storage of toys is simple. Since both baby and toys stay where they are put, you can arrange toys to suit your needs. Often the infant's toys are arranged attractively on a bureau. The arrangement is aesthetically pleasing to adults and easily restored should something be taken down to use.

Frequently toys are placed in the baby's crib. This is fine when the crib is being used as a play area, but I would

strongly recommend the removal of toys when the baby goes to sleep. Infants do not need the comfort of a stuffed animal or doll. Toys and stuffed animals represent a safety hazard when left in cribs overnight.

## Shelves

As the child gets older and can move around by himself, he is most likely to play with what he can see and reach. Low sturdy shelves are the best device for the display and storage of toys for children between the ages of eight months and five years. The shelves should not be higher than three feet since children will not be able to reach what they see. The shelves must be sturdy because children will climb on them—especially if they are taller than three feet and a desired item is on a high shelf. I observed a two-year-old use the drawers of her dresser as a ladder in order to reach a desired item on top of the dresser.

The shelves should have vertical dividers so that sections can be designated. Although children may not put everything back exactly where it belongs, they will begin to develop a sense of order—e.g., books in one section, puzzles in another. This helps children classify toys into categories and makes restoring order a less arbitrary and overwhelming task. If books always go in a certain spot, the child does not have to decide where to put them. For the two- to four-year-old such decisions often make the task of restoring order too difficult.

## Toy Boxes

Toy boxes are often placed in children's bedrooms. They are large, can hold many toys, and seem practical from the adult's perspective. They are not particularly useful from the child's vantage point. If the toddler is strong enough to lift the lid, he is rarely wise enough to angle it so that it stays open. Inside he finds a jumble of toys and hardly ever gets beyond grabbing something from the top layer. If a toy has loose pieces, they invariably fall to the bottom of the toy box, not to be seen again until you clean out the box. Toy boxes increase the child's inclination to "dump" and throw toys. This increases the number of broken toys.

## Closets

One of the least efficiently used resources in a child's room is his closet. Most frequently the closet is used in a manner similar to a toy box—that is, the floor becomes a jumble of toys. The construction of a few simple shelves of various widths can dramatically increase toy storage space. Nowadays children of either sex have few items of clothing that need to be hung, and even a few special items rarely need more than two feet of hanging space. That leaves four feet from the floor to be used for shelves. Two or three shelves can easily be constructed. It is useful to have a wide bottom shelf (approximately eighteen inches) to hold large toys for young children and later to hold the many board games of the older child. Sometimes shelves can be added above the rod or on the side of the closet. Since these shelves are not easily accessible and are beyond the reach of the child, they should be used only for storage purposes. Toys that are not currently favored by the child can be put away and reintroduced several months later. They will be received by the child with the same enthusiasm evoked by a new toy.

## Shoe Bags

As children get older, their toys have more little parts. Keeping the pieces together so that the toys remain intact is a chore. Recycled shoe boxes, coffee cans, and plastic containers are helpful. My favorite solution to the problem, however, is the use of shoe bags. Today, children's shoe bags are brightly colored, attractively designed items. They have anywhere from six to twelve pockets and a hanger that allows them to be hung on any convenient doorknob or hook. Children can stuff a wide variety of toys in the pockets—little people, little cars, plastic soldiers, firemen, cowboys, Indians, and so on. They are the perfect storage place for the four-year-old's treasured collection of rocks, marbles, seashells, jewelry, baseball cards, or whatever is his current passion. Each pocket is large enough to hold a substantial number of items but small enough to assign one pocket for one purpose and maintain a neat system that makes cleanup easier. Children can easily see the contents of each pocket, and the arrangement encourages rather than discourages the use of toys.

## Beds

Children's furniture has become as varied in style, quality, and price as furniture for the living room. I will not begin to evaluate the available options, but I will make one suggestion for those instances when space is extremely limited and every available nook and cranny needs to be utilized. A captain's bed is a useful space-saving option. The base of the bed is a large box. The mattress sits on top and drawers occupy the space under the mattress. No box spring is needed. This type of bed allows you to use the space usually lost under the bed. The drawers are ideal for storing old or infrequently used toys.

## Crates

Recently, brightly colored plastic crates modeled after the old milk carton have become available. Several boxes placed next to each other can form a wall system for the display and storage of toys. Each box is approximately ten by ten by fifteen inches, inexpensive, brightly colored, and attractive. They are large enough for a child to sit in, sturdy enough for him to climb on, and, when empty, light enough for him to carry. When flipped over they can be used as a writing surface, desk, table, or chair. Their flexibility makes them particularly practical items to consider for use in a child's room.

Keep in mind that shelves can be added to any closet, a shoe bag hung on any doorknob, or a plastic crate placed unobtrusively in any corner of the home.

## The Kitchen

The kitchen is the busiest room in the house. It is also

one of the most interesting rooms to the young child. He can always find something to play with and is fascinated by the equipment we take for granted. Pots, pans, measuring cups, measuring spoons, sifters, colanders, and small canned goods are just a partial list of the items he will find interesting.

Unfortunately, the kitchen is also one of the most hazardous rooms in the house for young children. Household cleansers and detergents are poisonous if ingested. Sharp or pointed objects can cause cuts or puncture wounds. Glass jars and dishes are hazardous because they break easily. Before establishing a toy center in this room of the house, parents must be sensitized to the hazards that exist for the young explorer.

The young child is motivated to explore everything. This desire to know and to learn about the things in his environment is a positive characteristic that should be supported. However, curiosity can create problems for both parents and child. The child does not have the knowledge to discriminate between acceptable and unacceptable objects for exploration. He sees something that attracts his attention, and touching it is the obvious next step. The child under two does not have the self-control necessary to limit his explorations.

The safest and easiest strategy to adopt with the child under two is to "childproof" the kitchen. I have observed parents using other strategies such as constant vigilance or saying no and trying to redirect their child when he explores inappropriate items. These two strategies are time-consuming, frustrating, and exhausting. The parents find themselves with no time to do anything but watch the toddler. Even in a childproofed environment you will spend a great deal of time monitoring the child's activities, but constant vigilance or saying no and expecting a child under the age of two to obey also require a tremendous amount of effort and are usually unsuccessful. I observed one mother who decided to teach her child not to touch the dials on the television set. She devoted two days to the effort, saying no each time the child went near the dials. She reported that in two days she said no 230 times, but her eighteen-month-old still went back to the television dials on the third day.

The most effective strategy when a child is under two is to rearrange the contents of the kitchen so that all low cabinets contain items the child can explore and enjoy safely. All cleansers and detergents should be moved to a cabinet high enough to be inaccessible to the child. All breakable and sharp items should be moved beyond the reach of the toddler.

It is important to periodically reassess the location of potentially harmful items. As children learn to climb, what was inaccessible may become easily accessible. Be particularly conscious of where you store treats such as cookies. A child is likely to be tempted to climb up to a cabinet where sweets are stored and while there explore the other contents.

Some parents, instead of rearranging the contents of their cabinets, try to restrict access to the cabinets by tying or locking them. This tends to be risky because it is easy to forget to retie or lock a cabinet during a busy moment. In my opinion it is easier and safer to rearrange the contents of cabinets.

The kitchen is a natural habitat for young children, and utensils, pots, pans, lids, and canned goods all qualify as interesting "toys" for the young child. Some parents designate one cabinet for the child's use, and this toy center stores a conglomeration of household objects and toys. Other parents make no special designation and allow the natural contents of the room to serve as toys for the young child. Either strategy is successful with the child under the age of two. Do whichever feels more comfortable to you.

For the older child the kitchen is the ideal location for an arts and crafts toy center. Creative projects often require water, and spills, spots, and drips cannot be avoided. One drawer or cabinet can store paper, paint, paintbrushes, markers, glue, scissors, and clay. In addition, store one inexpensive plastic tablecloth with the supplies. This tablecloth can be spread out before the activity begins. It protects your table and makes cleaning up less of a chore.

## The Bathroom

Bathtime is a favorite activity for most children, and toys quickly accumulate in this room, too. Storage problems can easily be solved by storing toys in a large plastic pail (the handle allows you to hang the contents in the tub) or in a large net shopping bag. The net bag, usually sold in a dime store, takes up less space than the pail and expands and contracts with the amount of toys stored in it. Also the child can easily see the contents of the bag without pulling out every toy.

Children between the ages of ten months and two years find the bathroom fascinating. Although there are many intriguing activities for the toddler (water play, flushing the toilet, unwinding the toilet tissue), the potential hazards are numerous, and it is one room which is almost impossible to make safe for the young child. Falls from climbing in and out of tubs, accidental burns from hot water, and accidental poisonings from ingesting contents of medicine cabinets are some of the hazards. I strongly recommend keeping the door closed when the bathroom is not in use and limiting access to that room to times when you are also present.

## Dens, Family Rooms, Living Rooms

As your child gets older you can assign different categories of toys to different rooms of the house. For example, board games require the participation of two or more people and can easily be stored in a drawer in a family room where members of the family gather. Noisy toys should be stored in the child's bedroom where they are less likely to disturb others. Building toys require a hard surface and should be stored in a room with a flat rug or no rug at all.

The purpose of toy centers is to maximize the child's access to his toys, to increase his use of toys, and to increase the ease with which order can be restored. Periodically you should review the contents of the toy centers. Toys that are not used should be removed and stored. These toys can be reintroduced at a later date. As the child gets older, the number of toys he has increases greatly. Before birthdays and holidays it is a particularly good idea to go through the present stock and remove those toys he has outgrown or rarely uses. This makes room for the new additions and perpetuates the service-ability of toy centers in your home.

# XI

# Books

Storytime is one of the most cherished memories of childhood. For both the child and the adult, there is the pleasure of sharing in laughter, the opportunity to explore feelings and ideas, and the excitement of meeting people and places that exist beyond the confines of one's neighborhood.

Each year 3,000 books are published and added to the current list of 150,000 titles in *Children's Books in Print*. Choosing the right book for a child is not an easy task. Children's interests and attention span vary dramatically, and what appeals to one child may never be right for another. However, if you understand the development of language skills and couple this knowledge with criteria for selecting books, you will increase the likelihood that the book you choose will delight the children on your gift list.

## The Development of Language Skills

The ability to understand language begins between seven to twelve months of age. Although children cannot yet use language to express their thoughts, feelings, or needs, they are beginning to associate labels with objects and names with people. The first words they understand are the ones we use every day: Mommy, Daddy, spoon, cup, bottle, bye-bye. The child's ability to understand language grows rapidly during the next two years, so that by the age of three the child will understand most of the words used in everyday adult conversations.

The ability to speak emerges at widely disparate ages. Some children are talking in words or phrases at eighteen months while others barely say a recognizable word at two. A child's ability to use language is not critical in these early years. What is important is that her ability to understand words and follow directions clearly expands. The quantity and quality of language experience you provide for the child influences the development of this critical ability.

Storytime is an important part of the language experience you should provide for a child. For the eight- to twelve-month-old, storytime is a brief, fast-paced episode. The most appropriate books for children in this age range are stiff-paged picture books that depict familiar objects and animals. The eight- to twelve-month-old will want to explore the book in the same manner she would explore any other interesting object; she will mouth it, feel it, bang it, and carry it with her as she moves around the house. The best way to "read" to a child in this age range is to simply supply the appropriate labels for the pictures she is looking at. At this young age, she will rarely have the patience to listen to a short story.

By eighteen months, the child's attention span will increase slightly and her ability to understand words will increase dramatically. Eighteen-month-olds delight in simple stories with one main idea that have repetitive, rhyming texts. They vary in their ability to sit and listen to a story, and you must be aware of the child's mood and attention span when selecting a book. A highly active child who cannot stand still long enough for a quick hug will not be able to sit through a story that has more than one sentence on a page.

By two, most children use single words, others use phrases, and some talk in paragraphs. All are eager to master the use of language, and stories are a natural extension of this interest. The child will eagerly point to illustrations, demanding labels for the objects she sees and mimicking the words you supply. Children in this age range enjoy books that describe the adventures of children or animals in childlike roles. The child will absorb the words to her favorite story and enjoy providing the last word in the sentence or repeating a common refrain.

By three years of age, the child's ability to listen to stories increases, and she is ready for books with longer texts and more complex themes and plots. Many children in this age range enjoy listening to stories that explore feelings that they are experiencing but still not articulate enough to express themselves (e.g., jealousy, fears). Action is still important, and the child delights in following a favorite character through escapades depicted in a series of books. Madeleine, Curious George, and Babar are just a few characters who seem to capture the imagination of the three-year-old. Often she will memorize a book in its entirety and "read" it back to you. If you're not sure how much of her favorite book a child has absorbed, try skipping a page or changing the sentences. I am confident you will be corrected.

By age four the child begins to appreciate the humor and absurdities found in her books and rediscovers old favorites from this new vantage point (e.g., Richard Scarry's *Cars and Trucks and Things That Go*). As she enters the more peer-dominated culture of nursery school, a four-year-old begins to appreciate stories that detail struggles centering on friendship, jealousy, and feelings about being left out of the group. Even though she may begin to question the reality presented in her storybooks (e.g., can a dog really be as big as a house?) she still enjoys tall tales.

Children develop special interests between the ages of four and five, and books are a natural resource for expanding these interests. Topics such as dinosaurs, space travel, cowboys and Indians, and pioneers are discussed at a level that four- and five-year-olds can understand and enjoy.

## Reading to a Child

Educators report that children who are read to regularly during the first five years of life have fewer reading problems when they enter school. Storytime should be an opportunity for a child to have your undivided attention. Select a time when you are least likely to be interrupted by telephone calls, cooking food, or another child. A private storytime may be particularly reassuring to the child who is coping with the presence of a younger sibling. By establishing storytime as a priority in your day, you are communicating the high value you place on this important activity.

Some families regularly read to a child before bedtime. This is often a good strategy if the child is very active and finds it hard to sit still when her energy level is high during the day. A quiet time before going to sleep is the perfect time for a good story and a delightful way to end her day. But I would also suggest trying to incorporate a story into the pattern of your day so that the child begins to think of books as one of the many options available when selecting what to do next. Often the child will bring a book to you when she needs a change of pace. Listening to a story means cuddling close to you. It is a special time for quiet sharing and provides a break in what might otherwise be a hectic day for both adult and child.

Storytime should be a positive, warm experience, not something that is imposed on the child. Be flexible. If the child turns storytime into a "talking" or "game" time, try reading again later.

## Selecting Books

These five guidelines should make it easier for you to select appropriate books.

**1. Read the book before buying it.** Books not only tell stories but communicate morals, values, and role expectations. When selecting a book for a child it is important to consider the implicit values that are being communicated. Ask yourself whether they are consistent with the values you want to transmit to the child.

**2. Look at the illustrations.** Illustrations are a critical element in a child's book. For most children under five years of age, it will be some time before they learn to decode words. The illustrations are their way of deciphering the story and "reading" the contents of their books. For the youngest child, the illustrations are more important than the text. Illustrations can be effective whether they are in color or in black and white. Each picture should tell a story. The pictures should be clear, representing the scenes and action described in the text.

**3. Find out who the main characters are.** Children enjoy books populated with characters with whom they can identify. Whether the characters are people or animals, family constellations seem to be the most intriguing for children. Children like to see childlike characters solve their own and others' problems. In most books the central character is male. All children, but especially girls, should be exposed to books in which the central character is female. Madeleine and Frances are two heroines whose escapades will intrigue and delight children of both sexes.

**4. Determine whether the problems or adventures are easy for children to identify with.** Plots do not have to be realistic, but the theme of the book should deal with issues the child can recognize, such as jealousy, fears, sharing, and helping others.

**5. Decide whether you enjoy the story.** Some books become immediate favorites and others grow on children gradually, but you will be the one who must read the story over and over again. A well-written story will charm you as well as your child.

## Hardcover Versus Paperback Books

Children's books can be purchased with cloth, vinyl,

stiff cardboard, or paper pages. Cloth and vinyl books are presented as "first" books for babies. They are not useful. An infant does not look at books. For the eight-month-old, a cloth book is difficult to manipulate. The pages become a fistful of material in her tight grip. Stiff cardboard pages are excellent for the eight- to twelve-month-old. They are strong enough to withstand the everyday abuse of a child of this age and easy for the young child to manipulate. However, only the simplest of stories are published in this manner, and as soon as the child is ready for more interesting stories, you should move on to regular books.

Traditionally, hardcover books were considered best for young children. The bindings are stronger and tend to last longer than those on paperback books. However, the cost of hardcover books has risen greatly in the past few years and the number and quality of children's books published in paperback have also increased greatly. The cost of a paperback book is less than half that of a hardcover book. (In 1978 paperback prices ranged from $0.95 to $2.95 for a high-quality paperback book. Hardcover books of comparable quality cost between $3.95 and $6.95.) Although the bindings on hardcover books may last longer, the pages are equally fragile. Before buying a book, always check to see if it is available in paperback. With a little care, paperback books will last as long as you need them, and you will be able to provide more books for your money.

## Where to Find Books

In most cities it is not difficult to find a bookstore or large department store with a good selection of children's books. Some only stock books for adults, but these shops will have a copy of *Books in Print* and *Paperback Books in Print*, two reference texts that list all publications currently available. Each is cross-indexed so that you can locate a book by its author or by its title and indicates the publisher and the cost of the book. Your local bookstore should be able and willing to order any books you cannot find on the shelves. Other sources of children's books are as follows:

**Local stores**—Drugstores, supermarkets, and discount toy stores usually stock a small selection of inexpensive books.

**Book fairs**—Most public schools have a book fair at some point during the school year. The books are selected by the school librarian and, although most will be geared to the interests of the elementary school students, the fair will offer a small but excellent selection of picture books. A phone call to your local public school early in the school year will alert you to this event.

**Book clubs**—Adult book clubs offer opportunities to purchase children's books especially before the holiday season. They usually offer an excellent selection of high-quality books at discounted prices.

**Libraries**—Most libraries have a children's room or section stocked with a good selection of books. They usually allow a book to be borrowed for two to four weeks. This is ample time to find out if a particular book is one you want to purchase and add to the child's own collection. In addition, all libraries have the reference texts *Books in Print* and *Paperback Books in Print*, which will allow you to locate any book you may want to order.

## The Caldecott Medal

Each year a book is selected from the many new offerings to receive the highest honor for a picture book. The Caldecott Medal, awarded since 1938, honors the most distinguished picture book for the year and is presented to the illustrator. The award is made by a twenty-three-member committee consisting of children's and school librarians of the American Library Association. This "seal of approval" is indicative of the highest-quality available in picture books and provides a special treat for the reader. Recent recipients of this award are as follows:

1979 *The Girl Who Loved Wild Horses*
 by Paul Gable
1978 *Noah's Ark*
 by Peter Spier
1977 *Ashanti to Zulu: African Traditions*
 by Diane Dillon
1976 *Why Mosquitoes Buzz in People's Ears*
 by Diane Dillon
1975 *Arrow to the Sun*
 by Gerald McDermott
1974 *Duffy and the Devil*
 by Harve Zemach
1973 *The Funny Little Woman*
 by Blair Lent
1972 *One Fine Day*
 by Nonny Hogrogian
1971 *A Story—A Story*
 by Gail Haley
1970 *Sylvester and the Magic Pebble*
 by William Steig

## Our Favorites

The following books are the Kaban family favorites, and we hope they will give you as much pleasure as they have given us. The books are loosely organized according to their appropriateness for children from eight to sixty months.

*Early Words* by Richard Scarry
The bright, bold illustrations of familiar items make this a good choice for a child's first book. Its thick cardboard pages are strong enough to withstand the explorations of the very young child.

*Mother Goose* illustrated by T. Izawa and S. Hijikata
Mother Goose rhymes are available in numerous

books. This book, one of the Puppet Storybook series, contains twelve nursery rhymes. The illustrations are bold and bright and capture the essence of each rhyme. The contents and the stiff pages make this book particularly appropriate for the twelve- to eighteen-month-old child.

*The Three Little Pigs* and *The Little Red Hen* illustrated by T. Izawa and S. Hijikata

These books, also part of the Puppet Storybook series, offer excellent renditions of nursery tales in stiff cardboard-paged books. Nursery tales appeal to the youngest listener. The stories are simple, include repetitive refrains, and are filled with action.

*Goodnight Moon* by Margaret Wise Brown

This beautifully illustrated book is a perfect bedtime story for the twelve- to eighteen-month-old. The book contains a description, in rhyme, of the contents of the "great green room" and then says good night to each item in the room.

*Baby Farm Animals* by Garth Williams

This little Golden Book, with its appealing, gentle-looking illustrations of baby animals, is a good book for the twelve- to twenty-four-month-old. The text is brief and the book can be enjoyed without reading one word.

*Cars and Trucks and Things That Go* by Richard Scarry

This oversized picture book is full of delightfully illustrated real and fantasy vehicles. When we first purchased the book, we rarely read the text. We spent long periods looking at and naming familiar vehicles. The humor and absurdities depicted in the text and illustrations were appreciated more when we "rediscovered" this book when my children were around four years of age.

*Curious George* by H. A. Rey and Margaret E. Rey

The adventures of this appealing little monkey have been amusing children for decades. There are seven books in the series and each describes escapades that result from George's insatiable curiosity. The book *Curious George Goes to the Hospital*, written in collaboration with the Children's Hospital Medical Center in Boston, should be read to every child who has to be hospitalized.

*Madeleine* by Ludwig Bemelmans

Madeleine is one of the few female heroes found in picture books. Her adventures, told in rhyme, portray a determined, clever little girl who resolves dilemmas that baffle adults and children alike. There are five books in the Madeleine series, and all are fun to read and listen to.

*Where the Wild Things Are* by Maurice Sendak

When Max is sent to bed without his supper for acting like a "wild thing," his imagination transports him to the land where the wild things live. The magnificent illustrations dominate this book. Although the wild things are large and have fierce-looking appendages, they are easily controlled by Max. The brief text makes this an excellent book for the two-year-old but will delight older children as well.

*There's a Nightmare in My Closet* by Mercer Mayer

Many two-year-old children develop fears of the dark and are reluctant to go to bed. This amusing book describes how one little boy conquers his fear of what may be hiding in his closet at bedtime. The text is brief and a gentle accompaniment to the illustrations which so beautifully tell the story.

*Make Way for Ducklings* by Robert McCloskey

This book, awarded the Caldecott Medal in 1942, is beautifully illustrated and written. It is the story of two ducks who are looking for the perfect home to raise their young family in the city of Boston.

*The Story of Babar* by Laurent de Brunhoff

The series consists of more than fifteen books. The first book, *The Story of Babar*, begins when Babar is a little baby and describes his early adventures before becoming king of the elephants. The rest of the series describes the various adventures of King Babar and members of his family. The books are peopled with interesting characters from the mischievous Zephir the Monkey to the wise Old Lady who comes to teach the elephant children. Four recent additions to the series which are favorites in my house are *Babar Loses His Crown; Babar Comes to America; Babar's Birthday Surprise;* and *Babar Visits Another Planet.*

*Cat in the Hat* by Dr. Seuss

Dr. Seuss has written many books that delight children and parents. His imagination and ability to use language to amuse and hold the attention of children is superb. This book is one of our favorites. The rhyming text describes the chaos that results when the Cat in the Hat comes to visit Sally and her brother one rainy day.

*Katy No-Pocket* by Emmy Payne

This warm story of a mother kangaroo's attempt to find a solution to her lack of a pocket delights children of all ages.

*Harry by the Sea* by Gene Zion
illustrated by Margaret Bloy Graham

Harry is a little dog who innocently gets into trouble in much the same way as do many young children. Other books about Harry's adventures are *Harry the Dirty Dog* and *No Roses for Harry*.

*The Snowy Day* by Ezra Jack Keats

This beautifully illustrated book, one of the first to have a black child as its central character, was awarded the Caldecott Medal in 1963. It describes a small boy's adventure in the snow.

*Whistle for Willie* by Ezra Jack Keats

Learning to whistle is difficult but an accomplishment to be proud of when mastered. This book describes Pete's attempts to master this important skill.

*Blueberries for Sal* by Robert McCloskey

A warm delightful story of a little girl who loses her mother while picking blueberries but finds Mrs. Bear.

*George and Martha* by James Marshall

These five vignettes explore the friendship of two large hippos, George and Martha. The stories are amusing and touching.

*Yertle the Turtle* by Dr. Seuss

This book contains three stories with very clear morals at the end. Each story is delightfully told and illustrated.

*Bread and Jam for Frances* by Russell Hoban
illustrated by Lillian Hoban

The main character in this book and the others in the series is a delightful female badger named Frances. These stories are sensitive portrayals of the feeling and struggles that occur around issues such as eating, bedtime, the arrival of a new baby, and establishing friendships. Frances's wise parents always know what to say and do to help her solve her problems. Every book in the series is a gem. They are: *Bread and Jam for Frances; Bedtime for Frances; A New Baby for Frances; A Bargain for Frances;* and *Best Friends for Frances.*

*Lyle and the Birthday Party* by Bernard Waber
Lyle is a crocodile who lives with the Primm family in New York City. In this book Lyle is so jealous of Joshua Primm's birthday party that he becomes sick. Through a series of hilarious misunderstandings Lyle ends up in a children's ward of a large hospital. There are three books in the Lyle series and all are excellent.

*Eloise* by Kay Thompson
drawings by Hilary Knight
This book describes the escapades of six-year-old Eloise, who lives in the elegant Plaza Hotel in New York City.

There are many books to choose from when you are ready to introduce your child to the alphabet. Our favorites are:

*ABC* by Dr. Seuss
The rhymes and illustrations used to introduce each letter of the alphabet delight children.

*Curious George Learns the Alphabet* by H. A. Rey
Even while learning the alphabet, this curious monkey gets into mischief.

*The Sesame Street ABC Storybook* by J. Moss, N. Stiles, and D. Wilcox
illustrated by P. Cross, M. Frith, T. Hildebrandt, G. Hildebrandt, J. Mathieu, and M. Nadel
This oversized book, peopled with characters from the popular television show "Sesame Street," consists of a separate story for each letter of the alphabet.

# XII

# Toys to Take When Traveling

We all enjoy a change of scenery periodically. To a child, a trip to the supermarket can be as exciting as a vacation in a distant city. However, traveling can be an ordeal if adults do not carefully consider the constraints a trip places on the child.

Before deciding which toys to take, you must pack ample provisions of food, drinks, and snacks for the infant, toddler, or preschooler. A hungry or thirsty child cannot be distracted, regardless of how appealing a toy may be. Especially if you are traveling by air, anticipate delays, which may mean packing provisions for at least one extra meal. It is not wise to assume that the airline will stock milk, juice, or other supplies you may need. The best strategy is to be prepared for the worst.

Although parents are usually most reluctant to undertake outings with an infant, it is actually the easiest time to do so. An infant takes up little room and requires only three things to be happy: nourishment, a dry diaper, and you. Infants are invariably sturdier and more flexible than we imagine. Most will eat and sleep anywhere, and this is the one time when no toys are needed to accompany your child on an outing.

For the three- to seven-month-old child, the sights and sounds of new surroundings provide ample stimulation. In addition, his winning smile and generally pleasant disposition will invite interaction from other adults and

163

children. However, teething rings are useful when traveling with a child in this age range. Even while looking around, the child will find gumming on his favorite teether soothing. But be sure to bring along more than one. Invariably, the teether will fall at an inopportune moment and require a thorough rinsing before being returned to the baby's mouth. A replacement will give you some time and provide an interesting alternative for the baby to explore.

As the child grows, his needs expand, and your preparations for outings and trips must be more elaborate. Once the child crawls, he finds extended periods of confinement in high chairs, car seats, airplane, and bus or train seats tiresome. For a child, movement is an end in itself rather than a means of transporting himself from one location to another. When he cannot move about freely, he becomes restless and irritable. If your expectations are realistic and the toys you select appropriate for use in a limited space, the trip will be more pleasant for all concerned—you, the child, and the other passengers. A reminder: Do not let the child see or have all the toys at once. When traveling, it is important to preserve the novelty value of each toy you have selected.

For the one-year-old, pack a large plastic container filled with his favorite playthings. Toys such as small wooden blocks, pieces from the Fisher-Price Floating Family, and measuring spoons are good choices for a trip. Also include a stiff cardboard-paged book. This simple collection provides many different play options. A one-year-old child enjoys opening and closing the lid of the container as well as banging on the container as if it were a drum. In addition, he will be able to engage in his favorite activity: removing the contents from the container and putting them back in again.

Three blocks are sufficient for a trip. They make a delightful noise when shaken in the container and will satisfy the child's meager building needs. Pieces from the Fisher-Price Floating Family provide additional opportunities for the child to practice putting one object inside another. Measuring spoons are often a favorite possession because they can be mouthed safely, can be used for banging, and fit inside each other.

A stiff-paged book has multiple uses. The child will enjoy opening and closing the book as well as flipping the pages. The book also has pictures to look at and a brief story to listen to. Finally, it can serve as a screen for a game of "Hide the Block." Hide-and-seek games delight the one-year-old child and provide a novel approach for playing with a small sample of toys.

The eighteen- to thirty-month-old child is the most difficult to take on a trip. Walking, running, and climbing are such an important part of each hour for a child in this age range that confinement is a major hardship. In addition, he has little sense of time and cannot appreciate that he will be able to run about "soon." There are several strategies, however, that help to make traveling manageable.

Plan your traveling time around the toddler's nap time. This will make the trip seem shorter and, consequently, easier for the child to endure. Even if traveling by air or train, be prepared to walk around with the child. (On one air trip, I am convinced I actually walked from Boston to Florida with my son.) If you are taking a long car trip, make frequent stops and allow the child to run and play.

If the child already enjoys listening to stories, take along a selection of his favorite paperback books. If he has not yet shown the interest or the attention span necessary for listening to a story, select several books with excellent illustrations and very brief texts. Books are one of the best sources of entertainment for a child on a trip. In addition, paperback books are light and take up little space when packing.

If you have not yet introduced the child to crayons, a trip is the perfect time to do so. The excitement of exploring a new medium will intrigue and occupy him for extended periods of time. Although he will not make elaborate pictures, scribbling with different colors or drawing with you will please him immensely.

Another effective strategy is to have a surprise hidden in your bag. A new toy is exciting anytime but particularly useful during an extended period of confinement. Three excellent possibilities are provided by Fisher-Price: Play Family House Bath Utility Set, Play Family Nursery Set, and Play Family Little Riders, all described in chapter 4. Each set comes in a flat cardboard package, which makes it easy to pack, and each contains many little toys that appeal to a child in this age range.

Traveling with a preschooler is much easier than traveling with a toddler. Although he may not enjoy the physical constraints any more than the younger child, he will be excited about his destination and more understanding about the limits that must be placed on his behavior. When traveling with the preschooler, pack a separate bag just for his toys. The three-year-old child will be glad to let you carry it, but by the age of four, most children want to take charge of their own toy bag. Involve the child in the selection of toys to be placed in the travel bag, but guide his choices. Frequently, a child's initial impulse is to fill the bag with toys he has not played with in months or with stuffed animals that are too large and heavy for traveling. Suggest books and one small stuffed animal or doll. In addition, the following toys and arts and crafts materials are excellent traveling companions for the preschooler.

**Legos**—Fill a pint plastic container with Lego pieces. This handy building toy is perfect for traveling. The pieces snap together securely so that structures will not fall with each movement of the plane, car or train. Even with a relatively small number of pieces, the child will construct many interesting shapes and structures. At home or traveling, Legos are one toy the child will come back to again and again.

**Crayons**—Although most children prefer markers,

crayons are a better choice for a trip. Markers leave an impression on everything they touch, including skin and clothing. The close quarters of most traveling arrangements make them potentially troublesome. In addition, bored children have a tendency to engage in "body decorations" when using markers. Crayons do not write as well on skin and consequently discourage such creative explorations. If neatness counts, the child will look better when he arrives at his destination if he has been writing with crayons rather then markers.

**Paper**—Paper is compact and serves many purposes. In addition to using it for coloring, you can make paper hats, airplanes, and other original creations. A few sheets of colored paper as well as blank white pages provide variety and an added dimension to arts and crafts activities.

**Seals or Stickers**—Preschoolers love little pictures with gummed or self-adhesive backings which stick to paper, cardboard, or wood surfaces. Most books of seals have a common theme such as animals, flowers, sport scenes, or dinosaurs. "Holiday" seals are also popular. Eureka and Dennison offer a wide variety of packages ranging from thirty-six seals for $0.29 to fifty-four seals for $0.49. They are interesting "miniature" books for the preschooler to look at and offer many creative options for the young designer.

**Play Shapes by Patterson Blick**—These delightful precut self-adhesive shapes stick to most surfaces. They come in five bright colors and consist of circles, squares, rectangles, triangles, and other shapes in varying sizes. Each piece is easily dislodged from the sheet, and there are several hundred pieces in one package (purchasing price is approximately one dollar). The creative possibilities are endless; the child can construct random designs or make elaborate birds, trucks, houses, or people.

**Coloring Books**—Many adults, due to a fear of stifling creativity, avoid purchasing coloring books. As with any toy, a child will enjoy coloring books if he is allowed to experiment and use it in his unique manner. For some unknown reason, when outlines of realistic objects are drawn, adults feel compelled to comment that trees are not blue or that hair is rarely purple. Children recognize the differences between their pictorial representations and the real objects but do not feel bound by these constraints. Today, coloring books are designed to appeal to a broad range of interests in preschoolers. Superheroes, Sesame Street characters, and Disney characters are just a few of the new additions you will find in coloring books.

**Dot-to-Dot Books**—If a preschooler can count and recognizes numbers, Dot-to-Dot books are challenging and fun. Each picture consists of a numbered sequence of dots that form a picture when connected. This task is excellent for reinforcing number concepts as well as practicing the hand-eye coordination necessary in writing. Dot-to-Dot activity pages can be found in many coloring books.

**Wet-a-Brush Book**—This special type of coloring book offers the added dimension of "painting" without paint. A wet paintbrush applied to the surface of the picture results in the appearance of colors. The magical quality of this activity makes it particularly appealing to the preschooler. Although potentially messier than coloring, this book is an excellent choice for long air trips. Keep the amount of water the child has in a cup at a minimum and little damage will result should it spill. The unique quality of this activity will intrigue and occupy the child for a considerable time.

**Board Games**—Preschoolers love board games and can play the same game over and over again. Unfortunately, most commercial games are too bulky to take along on a trip. Homemade versions are compact and have as much play value as the fancier commercial models. (For instruction on how to make your own board games, see chapter 8.)

**Action Transfers by Letraset Consumer Products—** Transfers are the latest craze in the four-to-eight-year age range. An action transfer is excellent for traveling because it is small, light, and inexpensive. It consists of a background picture (ranging in size from four by five inches to eight by eleven inches) and a printed film sheet of characters in various action poses. The child creates his own scene by placing the figures on the background sheet. This is accomplished by "transferring" the action figure from the film to the background sheet with a simple rubbing motion (a pencil, bobby pin, or any other convenient tool can be used successfully). For the four-year-old child, the process is much more intriguing than the product he creates. Scenes depicted are primarily action sequences concerning superheroes, although Letraset is beginning to expand the scenarios to include animals and other scenes. Considering the minimal investment required (ranging from $0.39 to $2.50), action transfers are a novel activity particularly suited to the constraints of traveling.

**Books—**Reading stories is one of the nicest ways to pass the time when traveling. However, if you are the driver it is not possible to read to a child too. An excellent solution to this problem is taping the child's favorite stories and records on a small cassette recorder. Most cassettes run for thirty minutes, which is ample for any preschooler. The child will enjoy listening to the stories over and over again as well as singing along with his favorite records.

Traveling is broadening for children just as it is for adults. With a little planning and the careful selection of toys, you can make traveling one more interesting and educational experience in the life of a child.

# Appendix

## Toy Manufacturers

Child Life Play Specialties, Inc.
55 Whitney Street
Holliston, MA 01746

Childcraft Education Corp.
20 Kilmer Rd.
Edison, NJ 08815

Creative Playthings, Trademark
of CBS Toys
41 Madison Avenue
New York, NY 10010

Eden Toys, Inc.
112 West 34th Street
New York, NY 10001

Hancock Associates
Hancock, NH 03449

Horseman Dolls, Inc.
200 Fifth Avenue
New York, NY 10010

Ideal Toys
184-10 Jamaica Avenue
Hollis, NY 11423

Kenner Toys
1014 Vine Street
Cincinnati, OH 45202

Lego Systems, Inc.
555 Taylor Rd.
Enfield, CT 06802

Marx Toys,
Lewis Marx & Co., Inc.
633 Hope Street
Stamford, CT 06904

Milton Bradley Co.
1500 Main Street
Springfield, MA 01101

Ohio Art Products
East High Street
Bryan, OH 43506

Parker Brothers, Inc.
50 Dunham Road
Beverly, MA 01915

Schaper Manufacturing Co.
P.O. Box 1426
Minneapolis, MN 55440

Steiff Animals
1107 Broadway
New York, NY 10010

## Source for Information About Federal Safety Regulations for Toys

Consumer Product Safety Commission
(Boston Area Office)
100 Summer Street
Boston, MA 02110

## Sources for Information About Children's Books

Children's Book Council, Inc.
67 Irving Place
New York, NY 10003

*Children's Books in Print*
New York: R. R. Bowker
(revised annually)

*Horn Book* Magazine
Park Square Building
31 St. James Avenue
Boston, MA 02116

*A Parent's Guide to Children's
  Reading*
by Nancy Larrick
New York: Bantam Books, 1975

## Sources for Information About Children's Television

Action for Children's Television
46 Austin Street
Newtonville, MA 02160

National Association for Better
  Broadcasting
2315 Westwood Blvd.
Los Angeles, CA 90069

## Catalogue Sources for Children's Records

Children's Book and
  Music Center
5373 W. Pico Blvd.
Los Angeles, CA 90019

The Children's Center
3 Maryvale Lane
Peabody, MA 01960

Children's Music and
  Book Catalogue
1201-C East Ball Rd.
Anaheim, CA 92805

# Index